Janet Sinder
Editor

Law Librarians Abroad

Law Librarians Abroad has been co-published simultaneously as *Legal Reference Services Quarterly,* Volume 18, Number 3 2000.

Pre-publication
REVIEWS,
COMMENTARIES,
EVALUATIONS . . .

"Janet Sinder's collection of articles recounting the adventures of *Law Librarians Abroad* not only provides great practical tips on how to practice our profession for fun and profit on foreign soil; it inspires us to expand our skills and our horizons to extend legal information services throughout the world."

Carol D. Billings, MA
Director
Law Library of Louisiana

More pre-publication
REVIEWS, COMMENTARIES, EVALUATIONS . . .

"*Law Librarians Abroad* is a pure pleasure! How rare to read a book about living and working overseas that is nonetheless professionally informative. This book is invaluable for those of us itching to live and work abroad and a delightful read for those of us wary of doing so, but who want to enjoy the experience vicariously. Law librarians seeking information on how to find professional work abroad and useful advice on how to survive in a foreign land will be amply rewarded."

Peter C. Schanck, JD, MLS
Law Library Director
and Professor of Law

"In *Law Librarians Abroad*, you may well experience the 'euphoria . . . depression . . . and equilibrium' that accompanies overseas assignments. And, if you find these experiences powerfully inviting, as do I, our adventurous colleagues provide a helpful guide to satisfy our yearning. Moreover, these stories offer a delightful, refreshing tonic to those for whom taking an extended leave is just out of the question. This is an insightful how-to-do-it travelogue for librarians with a pleasing balance between professional observations and personal experiences."

Roger F. Jacobs
Associate Dean for Library
and Information Services
Professor of Law
Notre Dame Law School

The Haworth Information Press

Law Librarians Abroad

Law Librarians Abroad has been co-published simultaneously as *Legal Reference Services Quarterly,* Volume 18, Number 3 2000.

The *Legal Reference Services Quarterly* Monographic "Separates"

Below is a list of "separates," which in serials librarianship means a special issue simultaneously published as a special journal issue or double-issue *and* as a "separate" hardbound monograph. (This is a format which we also call a "DocuSerial.")

"Separates" are published because specialized libraries or professionals may wish to purchase a specific thematic issue by itself in a format which can be separately cataloged and shelved, as opposed to purchasing the journal on an on-going basis. Faculty members may also more easily consider a "separate" for classroom adoption.

"Separates" are carefully classified separately with the major book jobbers so that the journal tie-in can be noted on new book order slips to avoid duplicate purchasing.

You may wish to visit Haworth's website at . . .

http://www.HaworthPress.com

. . . to search our online catalog for complete tables of contents of these separates and related publications.

You may also call 1-800-HAWORTH (outside US/Canada: 607-722-5857), or Fax 1-800-895-0582 (outside US/Canada: 607-771-0012), or e-mail at:

getinfo@haworthpressinc.com

Law Librarians Abroad, edited by Janet Sinder, AB, JD, MS (Vol. 18, No. 3, 2000). *"A pure pleasure! Law librarians seeking information on how to find professional work abroad and useful advice on how to survive in a foreign land will be amply rewarded. Delightful." (Peter C. Schanck, JD, MLS, Law Library Director and Professor of Law, Marquette University Law Library, Milwaukee, Wisconsin)*

The Political Economy of Legal Information: The New Landscapes, edited by Samuel E. Trosow (Vol. 17, No. 1/2, 1999). *Through this informative book you will gain new insights in such important issues as how industry consolidation will effect small legal publishers and the possibility that the law that governs public access to judicial opinions mandates citation reform.*

Symposium of Law Publishers, edited by Thomas Woxland, MLS, JD (Vol. 11, No. 3/4, 1992). *"Librarians involved in collection development would find the symposium useful as it provides an insider's view of the legal publishing industry." (Canadian Law Libraries)*

The Legal Bibliography: Tradition, Transitions, and Trends, edited by Scott B. Pagel, JD, MLS (Vol. 9, No. 1/2, 1989). *"An excellent introduction to major bibliographic titles and future concerns for the novice law librarian or student of legal librarianship. . . . A useful addition to the reference shelf of the private law or acquisitions librarian." (Legal Information Alert)*

Practical Approaches to Legal Research, edited by Kent C. Olson, JD, MLS, and Robert C. Berring, JD, MLS (Supp. #01, 1988). *"A long overdue book–a legal research manual for librarians. . . . A readable and entertaining text on locating and using law books. . . . Almost everything a law librarian needs to know about legal research is covered in this book." (Legal Information Alert)*

Law Librarians Abroad

Janet Sinder
Editor

Law Librarians Abroad has been co-published simultaneously as *Legal Reference Services Quarterly,* Volume 18, Number 3 2000.

The Haworth Information Press
An Imprint of
The Haworth Press, Inc.
New York • London • Oxford

Law Librarians Abroad has been co-published simultaneously as *Legal Reference Services Quarterly,* Volume 18, Number 3 2000.

Cover design by Thomas J. Mayshock Jr.

Library of Congress Cataloging-in-Publication Data

Law librarians abroad / Janet Sinder, editor.
p. cm.
Co-published simultaneously as Legal reference services quarterly, v. 18, no. 3, 2000.
Includes bibliographical references and index.
ISBN 0-7890-1316-9 (alk. paper)–ISBN 0-7890-1317-7 (pbk. : alk. paper)
1. Law librarians–Employment–Foreign countries. I. Sinder, Janet. II. Legal reference services quarterly.
Z682.4.L37 L38 2001
026′.34–dc21 00-054223

Indexing, Abstracting & Website/Internet Coverage

This section provides you with a list of major indexing & abstracting services. That is to say, each service began covering this periodical during the year noted in the right column. Most Websites which are listed below have indicated that they will either post, disseminate, compile, archive, cite or alert their own Website users with research-based content from this work. (This list is as current as the copyright date of this publication.)

<u>Abstracting, Website/Indexing Coverage</u> . . . . . . <u>Year When Coverage Began</u>

- ***BUBL Information Service An Internet-based Information Service for the UK higher education community <URL: http://bubl.ac.uk/>*** **1994**
- ***CNPIEC Reference Guide: Chinese National Directory of Foreign Periodicals*** **1995**
- ***Current Awareness Abstracts of Library & Information Management Literature, ASLIB (UK)*** **1997**
- ***Current Cites*** **1992**
- ***Current Law Index*** **1992**
- ***FINDEX <www.publist.com>*** **1999**
- ***Hein's Legal Periodical Checklist: Index to Periodical Articles Pertaining to Law*** **1992**
- ***IBZ International Bibliography of Periodical Literature*** **1995**
- ***Index to Legal Periodicals & Books*** **1992**
- ***Index to Periodical Articles Related to Law*** **1992**

(continued)

- *Information Science Abstracts* **1992**
- *Informed Librarian, The <http://www.infosourcespub.com>* **1993**
- *INSPEC* **1992**
- *Journal of Academic Librarianship: Guide to Professional Literature, The* **1997**
- *Konyvtari Figyelo (Library Review)* **1992**
- *Library & Information Science Abstracts (Lisa)* **1992**
- *Library and Information Science Annual (LISCA) <www.lu.com/arba>* **1998**
- *Library Literature & Information Science* **1992**
- *Newsletter of Library And Information Services* **1994**
- *OCLC Public Affairs Information Service <www.pais.org>* **1992**
- *Sage Public Administration Abstracts (SPAA)* **1992**

Special Bibliographic Notes related to special journal issues (separates) and indexing/abstracting:

- indexing/abstracting services in this list will also cover material in any "separate" that is co-published simultaneously with Haworth's special thematic journal issue or DocuSerial. Indexing/abstracting usually covers material at the article/chapter level.
- monographic co-editions are intended for either non-subscribers or libraries which intend to purchase a second copy for their circulating collections.
- monographic co-editions are reported to all jobbers/wholesalers/approval plans. The source journal is listed as the "series" to assist the prevention of duplicate purchasing in the same manner utilized for books-in-series.
- to facilitate user/access services all indexing/abstracting services are encouraged to utilize the co-indexing entry note indicated at the bottom of the first page of each article/chapter/contribution.
- this is intended to assist a library user of any reference tool (whether print, electronic, online, or CD-ROM) to locate the monographic version if the library has purchased this version but not a subscription to the source journal.
- individual articles/chapters in any Haworth publication are also available through the Haworth Document Delivery Service (HDDS).

Law Librarians Abroad

CONTENTS

ABOUT THE EDITOR

Janet Sinder, JD, MS, is the Head of Information Services and Senior Lecturing Fellow at the Duke University Law Library. She also serves as the Web Site Manager for the Duke University School of Law. She received her JD from the University of Michigan Law School and her MS in Library Science from the University of Illinois at Urbana-Champaign. In 1996, Ms. Sinder spent time in Dublin, Ireland, researching Irish Legal History at Trinity College, Dublin. Each year she returns to Dublin to teach computer-assisted legal research to law students at Trinity.

∞ ALL HAWORTH INFORMATION PRESS BOOKS AND JOURNALS ARE PRINTED ON CERTIFIED ACID-FREE PAPER

Introduction: Law Librarians Abroad

Janet Sinder

Have you always wished you could work in a foreign country? Travel the world in search of the perfect law library experience (or the perfect wave)? For many librarians, working abroad is something they just dream about. All of the librarians who wrote articles for this book have made that dream a reality. But while they share this one trait, their experiences range widely, in length from a few weeks to many years, and geographically across every continent except Antarctica (we're still waiting for the first law library to be built there!).

The articles demonstrate that there are many ways to combine work and travel. Some authors went overseas as part of government programs, while others were on sabbatical, still others were retired, and some just picked up and went! It's also possible to work overseas in a position unrelated to the library; for example, Nancy Carol Carter has served as Director of her law school's summer programs and William Wells consulted about technology.

Reading these articles will allow you to do more than just some armchair traveling around the world. You can see how law libraries here in the U.S. compare to those overseas. It's also interesting to see how the typical law librarian's skills, honed in one country, will work in another. Not all of the authors in this issue are American–Pat Northey came all the way from New Zealand to work in the U.S. and shares her sense of what it's like to experience the "foreign" culture of the United States.

[Haworth co-indexing entry note]: "Introduction: Law Llibrarians Abroad." Sinder, Janet. Co-published simultaneously in *Legal Reference Services Quarterly* (The Haworth Information Press, an imprint of The Haworth Press, Inc.) Vol. 18, No. 3, 2000, pp. 1-2; and: *Law Librarians Abroad* (ed: Janet Sinder) The Haworth Information Press, an imprint of The Haworth Press, Inc., 2000, pp. 1-2. Single or multiple copies of this article are available for a fee from The Haworth Document Delivery Service [1-800-342-9678, 9:00 a.m. - 5:00 p.m. (EST). E-mail address: getinfo@haworthpressinc.com].

Are you the type of person who would enjoy the overseas work experience? All of the authors were asked to provide their tips for working overseas, and several also comment on what character traits make you a likely candidate to enjoy it. The trait most often mentioned is flexibility, and its value comes through in all of the papers. In almost every situation, the librarian was confronted with something that didn't work out as planned–organizations didn't function as anticipated, the job they thought they were going to be doing was completely different from what the overseas institutions expected, and so on, and so on. . . .

If, after reading this issue, you think you might be interested in pursuing your dream of combining work and travel, you'll find lots of tips on ways to get involved in a variety of projects overseas. In addition, David McFadden discusses AALL's Foreign and Comparative Law Special Interest Section's Clearinghouse for Internships and International Personnel Exchanges, and Muriel Efron lists information on a number of Law Librarians' organizations around the world that she found invaluable in obtaining positions overseas.

I hope you will enjoy reading about the varied experiences enjoyed by librarians all over the world. Bon voyage!

The Adventures of Two Librarians in Buenos Aires, Argentina, and Athens, Georgia, U.S.A.

Anne Burnett
Laura Martino

SUMMARY. As part of a project funded by a USIA grant, the two authors visited each other's libraries and worked on projects related to curriculum development in the area of alternative dispute resolution. In addition to describing their experiences, the article includes information on how librarians can become involved in projects such as this one. *[Article copies available for a fee from The Haworth Document Delivery Service: 1-800-342-9678. E-mail address: <getinfo@haworthpressinc.com> Website: <http://www.HaworthPress.com> © 2000 by The Haworth Press, Inc. All rights reserved.]*

INTRODUCTION

This article focuses on visits rather than on an actual exchange. We each visited the other's library for one month and worked together on projects, instead of the classic exchange involving trading places. These visits, and the resulting projects, were funded by a United States

Anne Burnett, JD, MLIS, is Foreign and International Law Librarian, University of Georgia School of Law Library, Athens, Georgia.

Laura Martino, Lic., is Director of the Biblioteca Central, Universidad del Salvador, Buenos Aires, Argentina.

[Haworth co-indexing entry note]: "The Adventures of Two Librarians in Buenos Aires, Argentina, and Athens, Georgia, U.S.A." Burnett, Anne, and Laura Martino. Co-published simultaneously in *Legal Reference Services Quarterly* (The Haworth Information Press, an imprint of The Haworth Press, Inc.) Vol. 18, No. 3, 2000, pp. 3-13; and: *Law Librarians Abroad* (ed: Janet Sinder) The Haworth Information Press, an imprint of The Haworth Press, Inc., 2000, pp. 3-13. Single or multiple copies of this article are available for a fee from The Haworth Document Delivery Service [1-800-342-9678, 9:00 a.m. - 5:00 p.m. (EST). E-mail address: getinfo@haworthpressinc.com].

Information Agency grant obtained by faculty and staff of the University of Georgia (UGA) School of Law. In addition to describing our visits and related projects, we will discuss some tips for visiting and hosting, along with ways in which librarians can become involved in similar projects.

THE GRANT

In the fall of 1997, Associate Dean Gabriel Wilner of the UGA School of Law and María Eugenia Giménez of the UGA International Development Office obtained funding from the United States Information Agency (USIA)[1] for a three-year project designed to give the law faculties of the UGA School of Law and the Universidad del Salvador (USAL) in Buenos Aires, Argentina, an opportunity to cooperate in teaching and curriculum development activities related to alternative dispute resolution. Faculty members from both institutions visit their counterparts, researching and teaching short courses in subjects related to dispute resolution. Associate Dean Wilner, along with USAL's Professor Eduardo Boneo Villegas, are serving as co-directors of the project while Ms. Giménez is coordinating the activities.

A discrete component of the nearly one hundred thousand dollar project focuses on cooperation between the law schools in exchanging information related to the grant's subject matter, alternative dispute resolution. To that end, the grant's co-directors and coordinator contacted the libraries of both institutions for advice on how best to accomplish this exchange of information. The important role played by libraries and librarians in the exchange of information soon became apparent to the grant's directors and the coordinator, and they asked that a librarian from UGA's School of Law travel to Buenos Aires and work directly with Laura Martino, the director of USAL's Central Library, on ways to develop the exchange of information between the two institutions. Consequently, Anne traveled to Buenos Aires in November 1998, and worked for one month with Laura and her staff. In June 1999, Laura traveled to Athens, Georgia, to work with the staff of UGA's Law Library on the grant and related projects. The staffs of both libraries continue to work on projects related to these visits and to the grant's objectives.

ANNE'S VISIT TO ARGENTINA

My visit went very smoothly, thanks to the planning of Laura, along with Mirta Barreiro and María Eugenia Giménez, International Development Officers for USAL and UGA, respectively. These three organizational dynamos arranged for my lodging and planned my activities during the month-long visit. Several weeks before my arrival in Buenos Aires, Laura e-mailed me to ask what I wanted to accomplish during my visit. Although a month may seem like a long time, the days and weeks go by very quickly, and we needed a plan to organize our time together. Since the main purpose of my visit was for us to spend time together brainstorming on ways for our institutions to exchange information and research related to alternative dispute resolution, the bulk of my time was reserved for discussion.

We agreed that training in researching the legal materials available in both countries was a first step in increasing our institutions' exchange of information. For that reason, I offered to provide training in the U.S. legal system, researching U.S. legal materials, and using the Web for legal research to the staff of the USAL Biblioteca Central. I provided similar training to USAL law students who were preparing to represent the United States in the 1999 Model OAS and to the members of RedAmicus, a consortium of private university librarians in Buenos Aires.

I received similar training in researching Argentine legal materials from USAL Reference Librarians and met with USAL's Legal Informatics Department for a demonstration of Sistema Argentino de Informática Jurídica, which is a subscription database maintained by the Argentina Ministry of Justice and is available on the Web.[2]

Early in our discussions, Laura and I decided that we wanted to produce a tangible result from our collaboration, and we focused on the dispute resolution aspects of MERCOSUR[3] in choosing a grant-related project. In searching the Web for more information, we found a dearth of primary sources relating to the implementation of the various agreements creating MERCOSUR. Consequently, we searched for a source for some of these materials with an eye towards mounting them on a Web site. Laura contacted Professor Moya Dominguez, a member of the USAL law faculty and a member of the Joint Parliamentary Commission on MERCOSUR, and began laying the groundwork for the Commission to supply USAL with documents related to dispute resolution in MERCOSUR. Laura discusses the progress of this project *infra*.

Although we did not yet have the primary sources we were seeking, I was able to work with USAL library staff during my visit to create the framework of our Web site on dispute resolution in MERCOSUR. The framework of the site is bilingual (English and Spanish), but most of the contents will be in Spanish. The site is mounted on the Web at <http://www.lawsch.uga.edu/lawlib/mercosur/mercosur_eng.html>.

My hosts at USAL were generous, warm, and made my visit pleasant and productive. Although my inadequate Spanish skills provided numerous obstacles, the USAL main library staff went to great lengths to help me overcome those difficulties. In particular, Laura spent many hours each week translating for me during training sessions and meetings. I was also amazed at how much these *porteños* (residents of Buenos Aires) know about the United States.

Other grant-related activities included meeting with the deputy secretary for cultural affairs (a USIA employee) at the U.S. embassy in Buenos Aires and visiting several libraries in Buenos Aires, including the Economics and Social Sciences library at the Universidad de Buenos Aires (UBA), the UBA Law Library, the Information Resource Center at the United States embassy in Buenos Aires, the Legislative Reference Library for Argentina's Congress, and the Argentina Library of Congress. UGA Law Library Director Ann Puckett was able to participate from afar when she assisted the USAL library in preparing their first self-evaluation by providing relevant library science publications and arranging for transmission of draft copies of the self-study recently completed by UGA's Law Library and Computing Services Department.

One of the wonderful side benefits of working in a foreign country for a few weeks is the opportunity to learn about it in a way unavailable to tourists. My previous exposure to Buenos Aires had been limited to TV documentaries about Eva Peron, Amnesty International letter-writing campaigns on behalf of "the disappeared," and Nancy Drew's adventures.[4] I was delighted to find that Buenos Aires is a cosmopolitan city, with an eclectic mix of Latin American, European, and modern architectural styles. My half-hour walk each way between my apartment and the library took me through the heart of Buenos Aires' downtown, allowing me to get a real sense of this bustling city. I stayed in a studio apartment, or "apart/hotel," called the Edificio

Arenales, near the large shopping district on Calle Florida. The accommodations were clean and nice, with a pleasant English-speaking staff manning the front desk. A small market just across the street, along with a modern supermarket two blocks away, provided convenient access to the essentials. Although I cooked and ate in my room frequently, I also took advantage of the plethora of excellent restaurants and cozy cafés on every block. As a vegetarian, I was a bit apprehensive about suitable dining in a country known for its beef production, but I was pleasantly surprised by the availability of delicious pastas and salads. I also enjoyed the common afternoon snack of good strong Argentine coffee along with dainty *medialunas*, or small croissants.

LAURA'S VISIT TO THE UNITED STATES

My visit to Athens presented many advantages as compared to Anne's: first, I had worked for a month with her in Argentina, so I already knew her. Second, I had much information about the United States and how academic libraries worked, because in many cases we use bibliographic material produced in the United States. Another advantage was that I am able to communicate in English.

Anne organized my schedule before my arrival; to that end, she first asked me what I wanted to accomplish during my visit. Since I wanted to get in touch with each area of the library, I met with the Library Director and interviewed library staff responsible for Reference, Collection Development, Public Services, Computing Services, Acquisitions, Cataloging, and Collection Management. This helped me to understand their policies and procedures. I was then able to analyze them from within the existing Universidad del Salvador framework.

Other activities that I carried out during my visit included: working with Anne on the Web project, receiving training in researching legal materials using Lexis, training Anne concerning Web resources for Argentine legal research as well as for the acquisition of Argentine materials, participating in some of the library staff meetings to understand the way they worked, and receiving training in the use of the Law Library's automation system. In addition, I met with Associate Dean Wilner and grant coordinator María Eugenia Giménez to flesh out further details on grant-related projects. I was also invited by the reference librarians to participate in their presentation at the Continuing Legal Education Program during the annual meeting of the State Bar in Savannah, Georgia. This was a very useful experience for me as an example of cooperation between the University and the professional community.

In addition, I spent two days touring the UGA Main and Science Libraries and meeting with librarians in several departments. Part of my time was also dedicated to bibliographic research concerning some projects in which I am involved.

In conclusion, I suggest that the activities in which you choose to become involved during an international visit depend on the interests or projects you may have. These visits are a great opportunity to see how people in very different environments, with very different resources, solve in different ways (not better or worse, just different) the same problems that you have. I was very fortunate to come to a place where people were very kind to me. This does not always happen, and it helped me very much. Disaster looms if the people who receive you do not want to cooperate, or if they find that your visit has no purpose. The objectives of the visits must be very well stated and must be clear for all the people and institutions participating in them.

I also recommend that you take adequate time to prepare for the visit. This means gathering information about the institution, the names and positions of the people who work there, and information about the town and the state. I found most helpful the information provided by USAL professors who had previously visited Athens. They gave me information of great value. For example, I had decided at first to go to Athens alone, but after meeting with Professor Moglia Claps who had visited Athens some months before, I decided that it was better that I travel with my husband and daughter. Athens in June is a very quiet place to be alone.

OUTCOME OF OUR PARTICIPATION IN THE GRANT (SO FAR)

Since Anne's visit to Argentina, when we decided to contact the Joint Parliamentary Commission of MERCOSUR, we have signed a cooperation agreement between the Argentine Parliament, UGA, and USAL as a the first step to publishing on the Internet the rules produced by the Commission. We have presented the project to the Commission's President and now are waiting for his approval.[5] The project involves the digitization of printed documents, the publication of a bilingual abstract (Spanish-English), full-text searching, and the possibility of retrieving documents by subject.

In addition, both libraries have increased their acquisitions of materials related to the objectives of the grant. Some of the grant monies have gone specifically to library acquisitions designed to support research in dispute resolution in the Americas. Both libraries will lend materials to each other's patrons, and, in support of the grant's objective to increase communication between the two schools, grant money is being used to purchase software that will enable the USAL library to mount its online catalog on the Web, thereby increasing accessibility by UGA's faculty and students to the USAL library holdings. UGA's catalog is already accessible through the Web at <http://lawlib.lawsch.uga.edu>.

WAYS OF BECOMING INVOLVED IN SUCH EXCHANGES

Grants

Grants from the government, corporations, and private foundations are viable sources of funding for exchanges. Determine if your institution or professional organization provides grants. For example, members of the Librarians Association of the University of California may apply for grants funded by the University of California Office of the President.[6] The American Library Association, in conjunction with USIA, formerly provided grants to Library Fellows expressly for the purpose of working abroad. The American Bar Association's Central and East European Law Initiative (CEELI) arranged for an Albanian librarian to visit the UGA Law Library in 1996. That visit led to a reciprocal visit by an American librarian.[7]

If you are at an academic law library, find out if librarians at the main library have participated in exchanges. Such discussions with Laura Shedenhelm of UGA's Main Library revealed that the ALA and USIA provided grant money for librarian exchanges up through the early 1990s, and Ms. Shedenhelm utilized one of these grants to spend a year in Honduras.[8]

Utilize any help that your institution provides regarding grants or exchanges. If you are at a law school with a development or grant office, obtain the assistance of that office. In addition, determine whether the university's main library has a development or grant officer who may be more familiar with funding sources for librarians' projects and research. These folks are professional grant-writers who can help you to identify possible funding sources and to prepare your proposals. For example, at the University of Georgia, development officers in thirteen schools coordinate grant-seeking activities. In addition, individual development offices, such as the Office of International Development, work to obtain grant monies to further specific types of projects. Thus, law librarians at the UGA Law Library can obtain advice and assistance from the Law School's Development Office, from the University Libraries' Development Office, and from the Office for International Development. At the University Libraries, Development Officers Chantel Dunham and Susan Landrum actively solicit proposals from librarians.[9] The office identifies family and corporate foundations that might be especially good sources of grants for specific library topics.

Partnering with Colleagues

Partnering with others in your organization will establish librarians as expert resources for technological and research components of grant-funded projects. Establishing yourself as an expert resource may place you on the A-list for participation in future exchanges.[10] Our opportunities literally fell into our laps, but without established relationships in our institutions, we would never have been approached about participating in this exchange.

TIPS FOR WORKING IN A FOREIGN COUNTRY

Check far in advance on vaccination and visa requirements.

Ask for recommendations on publications about the country you will be visiting so that you can familiarize yourself with the culture before your arrival. It will help you to become comfortable in your new surroundings much more quickly. In addition, become familiar with typical reactions to working abroad for extended periods, especially if planning an exchange of more than a few weeks.[11]

Learn the public transportation system early on so that you can travel efficiently throughout your host city. In Buenos Aires, for example, Anne asked about the safety and reliability of the Subte, their subway system, and was told uniformly that the Subte was very safe and reliable during the day, but not to ride it at night. Taxis were plentiful and inexpensive, making travel at night feasible.

Find out in advance where you'd like to travel outside of your host city. Although Anne had a couple of weekends free, she did not plan in advance and, therefore, was unable to take advantage of some of the great offers for travel throughout Argentina.

Determine which expenses will be covered and what types of documentation you must present for reimbursement. Develop a system for keeping these records. Keeping a daily log of expenses will make the process of filling out expense reports much easier.

Do not overestimate your stamina. Be sure to include plenty of down-time, as familiarizing yourself with new surroundings, colleagues, language, and work routines can be exhausting.[12]

COSTS AND BENEFITS TO PARTICIPATING LIBRARIES

All exchanges and visits involve some costs to the involved libraries. Anne's visit to Buenos Aires coincided with numerous year-end activities at USAL's Main Library. USAL staff time that otherwise would have gone to completing annual reports, budgets, requests for funds, etc., was devoted to hosting, training, and collaborative activities. In addition, work on the MERCOSUR Web site monopolized the library's one Internet workstation, which serves the entire library staff and any USAL faculty or students who come to the library for Web access. Both libraries had to compensate for the month-long absence of a librarian. This was especially burdensome for USAL's Main Library, which lost its director for a month! At UGA, other reference librarians had to cover Anne's shifts at the reference desk as well as assisting students with more involved foreign and international legal research problems. Before contemplating such a visit, consult with your colleagues to determine the consequences to them of a lengthy absence.

Along with the costs, however, participating libraries benefit from exchanges and visits beyond those benefits enjoyed by the individual traveling librarians. Meeting and working with colleagues from abroad provides differing perspectives about the same goals and obstacles. Our participation in this particular project is resulting in tangible benefits to both institutions in the form of funding for increased holdings in research areas supporting the grant's goals plus the upgrade of USAL's online catalog. The relationships formed by librarians in both institutions also opens the door to increased access by our patrons to the holdings in both institutions.

NOTES

1. Congress recently abolished the USIA and assigned many of its functions to other governmental entities. The State Department currently administers UGA's grant.

2. *Sistema Argentino de Informática Jurídica* at http://http://www.saij.jus.gov.ar (last visited March 26, 2000).

3. MERCOSUR is the Southern Cone Market comprised of Argentina, Brazil, Paraguay, and Uruguay. This customs union was created in 1991 by the Treaty of Asuncion (Treaty Establishing a Common Market), 30 I.L.M. 1041 (1991).

4. Carolyn Keen, *The Mystery of the Brass-Bound Trunk* (1976).

5. Recent presidential elections in Argentina diverted attention from these arrangements slightly and may delay some decisions. For more about the outcome of these elections, see *De la Rua Takes Over a New Argentina with Old Problems*, The Financial Times, Dec. 10, 1999, at 8.

6. *See Guidelines: University-Wide Research Grants for Librarians*, *at* http://www.ucop.edu/lauc/resguide.html (last visited Sept. 26, 2000).

7. In June of 1996, Elda Hoxha of Albania's Court of Cassation spent two weeks in training at the UGA Law Library with participation by Georgia State University's Law Library, the Georgia Court of Appeals, and the Atlanta law firm of Troutman Sanders. In early 1997, Suzanne Morrison, law librarian at the Eighth Circuit Court of Appeals, traveled to Albania to Assist Ms. Hoxha with the development of the law library at the Court of Cassation. *See Central and East European Law Initiative*, *at* http://www.abanet.org/ceeli (last visited Sept. 26, 2000) for more information about ABA/CEELI activities.

8. Ms. Shedenhelm's experience demonstrates the flexibility one may have to show to participate in such an exchange. Married with two small children, she worked during the day on automation and cataloging projects at the Central Library of the Universidad Nacional Autónoma de Honduras while home schooling her oldest child at night. Ms. Shedenhelm's husband stayed in the United states and cared for their youngest child. For an account of her experiences in Honduras, *see* Laura Shedenhelm, *A Library Fellow in Honduras: Automatización de la Colección Hondureña*, Papers of the Thirty-Ninth Annual Meeting of the Seminar on the Acquisition of Latin American Library Materials 297 (1994).

9. "If you bring us the meat of the project, including projected costs, required staff time, and equipment, we will help you package the proposal," offer Ms. Dunham and Ms. Landrum, who hold workshops on obtaining grants as part of the University Libraries' professional development activities.

10. Faculty members who interact with librarians have a better understanding of the librarians' functions and the value of their expertise. Gaby Divay et al., *Faculty Perceptions of Librarians at the University of Manitoba*, 48 Coll. & Res. Librs. 27, 32 (1987).

11. Laura Shedenhelm of the UGA Main Library found pre-viewing USIA videos about the emotional highs and lows of overseas assignments to be very helpful during her year in Honduras. The classic cycle of psychological and emotional highs and lows involves euphoria (new setting, new challenges), depression (nothing works, the "challenges" are overwhelming), and equilibrium (everything in stride, all problems are manageable if not completely solvable).

12. Remember this caveat also if you are ever hosting a visitor. When Elda Hoxha, law librarian for Albania's Court of Cassation, visited the UGA Law Library in 1996, the library packed far too many activities into her workday schedule. Mid-way through her second week, it became apparent that overloading her schedule resulted in diminishing returns.

Law School Abroad: Ghiberti to Guinness

Nancy Carol Carter

SUMMARY. With the appropriate planning and the right frame of mind, working abroad is both adventuresome and exhilarating. The author shares her learning and experiences in directing summer law programs in Italy and Ireland and offers some practical advice to those contemplating a foreign work experience. *[Article copies available for a fee from The Haworth Document Delivery Service: 1-800-342-9678. E-mail address: <getinfo@haworthpressinc.com> Website: <http://www.HaworthPress.com> © 2000 by The Haworth Press, Inc. All rights reserved.]*

One reason to work abroad is to gain appreciation for the ease of doing business in the United States. Learning patience is another. Yet another may be daily walks past some of the greatest treasures of the Renaissance, or the opportunity to live on the same quiet square that Oliver Goldsmith inhabited while a student at Trinity College, Dublin.

All four of these benefits, and many more, came my way in two different stints as a program director for the University of San Diego's Institute on International and Comparative Law. The Institute runs summer programs in Barcelona, Dublin, Florence, Paris, London, Oxford, and Moscow-St. Petersburg. I worked in Italy and Ireland as director of the Florence program in 1996 and the Dublin program in 1999.

USD's Institute recruits program directors and faculty from the

Nancy Carol Carter is Director and Professor of Law, Legal Research Center, University of San Diego.

[Haworth co-indexing entry note]: "Law School Abroad: Ghiberti to Guiness." Carter, Nancy Carol. Co-published simultaneously in *Legal Reference Services Quarterly* (The Haworth Information Press, an imprint of The Haworth Press, Inc.) Vol. 18, No. 3, 2000, pp. 15-24; and: *Law Librarians Abroad* (ed: Janet Sinder) The Haworth Information Press, an imprint of The Haworth Press, Inc., 2000, pp. 15-24. Single or multiple copies of this article are available for a fee from The Haworth Document Delivery Service [1-800-342-9678, 9:00 a.m. - 5:00 p.m. (EST). E-mail address: getinfo@haworthpressinc.com].

ranks of our own law school, but also hires from other law schools, including those in the countries where the summer program is offered. Our Institute director regularly canvases the law school to see who wants to work in a summer program abroad. I expressed interest and accepted an assignment as soon as I thought my absence would not adversely affect the library or delay important projects.

Academic librarians who are interested in a foreign work experience should be alert to similar opportunities within their own institutions (programs may originate outside the law school). Making your interest, enthusiasm, and availability known are essential first steps. Then package your skills. Although the organizers of a foreign educational program may initially think about hiring teaching faculty, librarians may offer more appropriate skills, including administrative ability, technological savvy, and the ability to organize service delivery.

The USD International Institute expects the director to do everything necessary within A.B.A. and institutional guidelines to ensure that students receive the legal education for which they have enrolled. Furthermore, the program director must arrange informal educational programs to introduce students to the local legal system and do whatever is possible to ensure that students have a productive and enjoyable experience. Being a program director has been compared with being the dean and sole administrator of a tiny law school. Duties cover the waterfront, from faculty liaison, to academic advisor, to facilities manager. The director ensures the educational integrity of the program, as well as making sure that chalk, erasers, and bluebooks are available.

Because these programs bring students from all over the United States to a foreign city, the program director also serves as a tour guide, guardian angel, den parent, money lender, truant officer, sleuthhound of lost property, and occasional hand-holder to the inexperienced and overwhelmed student traveler. Most students come to a foreign program after their first year of law school. A surprising number are traveling abroad for the first time. While most of these neo-globetrotters are adaptable and adventuresome, a few are affronted upon learning that the familiar comforts and conveniences of life in the United States are not universally available. They adjust with varying degrees of success, but in a short time the students develop a sense of camaraderie and one observes the bloom of new friendships and the occasional steamy summer romance.

One of the more rewarding duties with the USD programs is to arrange extracurricular activities to help students learn about the legal system of the host country. This brings the program director into contact with an array of foreign judges, lawyers, and government officials that one would otherwise be unlikely to encounter. I have met an Italian judge who handles Mafia trials in a specially barricaded and guarded courthouse, a Brooklyn-born Harvard graduate who is the only American woman practicing law in Florence, the youngest member of the Irish parliament, and a Dublin police inspector whose only experience with carrying a weapon was as a United Nations civil police volunteer in Bosnia. Lawyers and officials in both Italy and Ireland were generous with their time and remarkably willing to help educate a group of American law students and their program director about local legal practices.

Likewise, these programs put the director into close contact with faculty from various institutions. In just two experiences, I have worked with outstanding faculty members from several American law schools and the law faculty of Trinity College. Of course, working with colleagues from your own institution at one of these foreign programs brings your professional and personal relationships to an entirely different level. The expatriate situation encourages a reprise of college days. The faculty often shares informal meals cooked in rented spaces with inadequate kitchens and takes time for long evenings of conversation.

The key to the success of the USD foreign programs, I have learned, is the on-site administrative assistant. Each program hires a local person who knows the language and how to get things done in the local business culture. I can categorically say that my experience with the Florence program would have been a disaster without the savvy Australian-Italian assistant who guided me through the mystery of doing business in Italy. More than that, she helped me penetrate the mystery. This is what I learned: things get done at the last possible moment in Italy, or they don't. It is all the same to the Italians. In other words, compulsive planning and follow-through–always my forte and so key to insuring a result in the United States–amount to unrewarded excess in Italy. Planning assures nothing. Follow-through is the self-deluding activity of an uninitiated foreigner.

Despite an order for a telephone two months in advance, and the appropriate reminders, there was no office telephone when the Florence program started. Despite an even longer notice to the landlords of the exact day I would show up to organize the office, my assigned space was stacked floor to ceiling with chairs the day I arrived. Conversely, one of the designated classrooms had no tables or chairs.

I discovered that opening an Italian bank account is an excruciating experience. In the place of toasters or other lures for the new customer, Italian banks offer intimidating guards armed with submachine guns, chambered security entrances that could contain a plutonium leak, and bank officers who sigh meaningfully while reluctantly taking your deposit money.

Surprisingly, my experience in setting up a program in Ireland, where I could communicate with the purveyors of telephones and the handlers of money, was even more difficult than in Italy. In Ireland, the office reserved one year in advance was not made available when our summer program started (although it sat vacant and in plain sight). I worked from a table in a hallway for five days, carrying my "office" in a large straw bag. Once admitted to the rented office, there was another ten-day wait for an office telephone. The Irish, it seems to me from my very brief experience, are incapable of feeling chagrined about unmet promises of service or, indeed, any level of inconvenience to the consumer. With so much beguiling charm in the air, who needs to deliver the goods?

These stories illustrate some of the frustrations and benefits of working abroad. My experience demonstrates that the things we usually consider necessities of business life, such as an office with a telephone, are dispensable in a pinch. I learned that many of my techniques for getting a job done and for making things happen did not necessarily translate to a new setting. While gnashing my teeth over the difficulties, I could not help but be fascinated. The necessity of finding substitutes for my "business as usual" approach required me to learn more about my host country. I had to be observant and adaptive. After my experiences of working in foreign settings, I better understand why patience is considered a virtue and how the American became ugly.

When abroad, we see other ways to work, and, more importantly, we can observe and experience other ways to live. This inevitably leads to comparisons with work and life back home. My experiences still have me marveling at the incredible efficiencies and conveniences we Americans take for granted. After working in just two foreign countries, both progressive members of the European Union, I could become a spokesperson for the U.S. Chamber of Commerce. Whatever your doubts, believe this: *America works*! What I mean is that things literally work here–telephones and transportation systems, to name just two. And people work. You can get something done before 10:00 a.m., and you do not have to take account of a two-hour lunchtime hiatus. Although we see examples to the contrary, businesses in the United States generally provide the services they promise, and people generally do the jobs for which they are paid.

After living and working abroad, one returns with questions about the price we pay for our efficiency and productivity. Both Italians and the Irish profess admiration for our prosperity and that job-producing machine we call a national economy, but at the same time, they pity us. They believe that we waste a lot of time and a lot of life by pouring our souls into our work. Perhaps they have a point. Why has our average work week become longer–not shorter–during the past two decades? When working in Europe, it does not take long to realize that most Europeans regard our workaholism as misguided, if not downright foolish. They are much more willing to relax, to socialize, and to focus on creating an enjoyable existence. While so many Americans are completely wrapped up in their jobs, most of the people I met in my foreign experiences are more inclined to "work to live, not live to work." It is also true that many consumer goods are so out of reach for the average worker abroad that the striving to possess the latest product on the market is not quite as ingrained as in the United States.

In each instance, my stays were five to six weeks in duration. This is the easy way to work abroad. Organizing all the details of being away from home and absent from one's usual job is very manageable for this length of time. Every work situation is unique and the management of extended absences varies greatly. I only know that it is essential to have helpful and supportive co-workers, as I am fortunate to have at the University of San Diego, and to bring them into your plans as early as possible.

PERSONAL CONSIDERATIONS AND PLANNING

Working abroad is not for everyone. Unfortunately, some people do not realize this until they have signed on for a foreign job and find themselves miserably unhappy, but obligated. The following thoughts are intended to help those considering foreign assignments to make a hard-nosed assessment of their aptitude for work abroad and what it takes to organize a relatively stress-free absence. I do not mean to discourage anyone, but to offer some realism and practicality. Many of these ideas will be familiar to experienced travelers, but they may be helpful to those just beginning to explore the other side of the rainbow.

The ideal candidate for a foreign work experience is a physically healthy person who feels that "home is where they hang their hat." The more comfortable and relaxed you are in new settings, the better. It is simply not feasible to take many familiar possessions along on this kind of trip (unless, of course, you are taking a long-term position with an employer who is funding a household move). For most experiences, the ideal is to take only the luggage you can personally handle and keep under your control. This usually means two bags or less.

If you are genuinely adaptable to different living conditions and unwedded to your possessions, a foreign work experience is much easier. If a television or a computer are home life essentials, living abroad may not be for you. Most of the rental apartments will not have televisions and even a laptop cannot be operated without purchasing the appropriate adapters and transformers for the local electrical current. Technology prices are sky high in Europe and many other countries; purchasing a television or a computer locally would be out of the question for most of us. Cyber cafes are becoming ubiquitous, but they are quite expensive. A small international shortwave radio might be a good investment if the length of your stay abroad justifies the expense, and particularly if you are a news junkie. Books also are expensive abroad, so it is a good idea to pack fat paperbacks that you can toss or trade after reading.

You should take a full supply of any prescription medications and extra pairs of glasses or contacts. Unless you are prepared to spend a lot of money on your wardrobe, you must take along all the clothing you expect to need if working in Europe, Japan, and similar economies. By American standards, men's and women's clothing is shockingly expensive and the selection is quite limited. (Yes, this is also true in fashionable Italy.) In fact, we are so spoiled by our relatively low cost of living that almost everything seems very expensive in other economically advanced countries.

Before going abroad to work, it is useful to accumulate as much liquid cash as possible. While having an amount of money over and above your expected needs is not an absolute necessity, it buys a lot of peace of mind. It is reassuring to know that you can meet emergencies and enjoy an occasional splurge during your overseas adventure. When you actually go abroad, do not depend entirely on one source of money–plan to take some cash, some traveler's checks, and a credit and cash card (check with your bank for an international pin number).

Unless you have a house-sitter and someone who will handle all your personal business in your absence, start your list-making at least three months in advance to document all the matters that will need attention in your absence. Figure out how your rent or mortgage and any other monthly obligations will be paid, what you need to do about utilities, and how your mail will be handled. Do you have quarterly or semi-annual financial obligations that will come due in your absence? The most conscientious among us will write a will and otherwise organize our personal affairs at this juncture.

Do you need to store an automobile? I use street parking at home, but by making prior arrangements was able to leave my vehicle in a university garage. An accommodating co-worker started the engine on a weekly basis. How about pets or plants? Most of my house plants went out to a shady place in the yard, to be watered by a neighbor. But I had to make special arrangements for "Sweet Fern," an asparagus fern that has lived with me for almost 30 years. She was the house guest of two very indulgent friends during my absence.

My point is, even if you live a relatively simple life, you need to plan well ahead for an extended absence. There may be much more to arranging a worry-free stay abroad than occurs at first blush. You cannot do everything the night before boarding an international flight, and it is extremely difficult to handle personal business matters once out of the country.

Make every effort to build in some free travel time before or after your work obligation. It may not seem vital since you will be living in the country, but you are likely to be frustrated at having to work during the entire duration of a stay in an interesting place. If you can plan additional travel at the end of your job, you will have learned about places off the beaten path, and by then you may know locals who will arrange visits to their family and friends in other areas of the country.

Those considering work in a foreign country should realistically reflect on their tolerance for the different and the unfamiliar. If any corner of your mind expects things to be the same in another country as at home, put that notion aside. *Nothing* is the same, no matter how familiar it may look from this distance. O.K., England is not Outer Mongolia, but trust me, it is also not Kansas. London is not Chicago or New York City.

In another country, you will not be able to replicate your usual diet. You may eat some of the same things, but they will have a different taste. You are unlikely to spend your work time or your leisure time in familiar ways. Almost nothing will operate in an accustomed manner. Are you willing to relearn the simplest tasks, like how to use a public telephone? Can you adapt to public transportation if you are not used to it? Can you live without a car and a telephone? Can you tolerate infrequent contact with family and friends? (Having e-mail in your foreign job can mitigate this problem, but you cannot automatically expect a web connection as you might in most U.S. jobs these days. As mentioned, cyber cafes are quite expensive, though telephone rates are dropping.) If you are a bit nervous, but still game, it might be a good idea to test your adaptability with a brief foreign work assignment. If anything in this list arouses your anxiety instead of your curiosity, you probably will be happier if you remain comfortably at home.

On the other hand, if you have a few ounces of adventure in your bones and several pounds of flexibility at your fingertips, there is nothing as interesting and exhilarating as the experience of working abroad. My own foreign work experiences were as enriching and enjoyable as anything I have done in the past few years.

THE GOOD LIFE IN FLORENCE AND DUBLIN

Remember, gainful employment in another country means that you have transcended the status of tourist! Even though free time is restricted by work, the experience is far superior. As tourists, we rarely settle down in one foreign city for an extended stay, and it is almost impossible to move beyond superficial interactions with local people. We may see all the sights and catch glimpses of everyday life in the places we visit, but that does not compare with the experience of settling into an apartment, shopping locally, and figuring out how to dispose of the household garbage. Without working in Florence, I could never have had the experience of living in a building that dates back to the 14th century. I am unlikely to have another bedroom with hand-painted cherubs flying about on the ceiling.

Despite my limited progress in learning basic Italian, within a few days I felt comfortably a part of my new neighborhood, buying cheese and olives from the man downstairs, bread at the corner bakery, and Milano salami from the store with the stuffed pigs out front. After the first week, the people at the newsstand whipped out my daily *International Herald Tribune* when they caught sight of me. I developed a nodding acquaintance with the elderly Franciscan brother I passed each morning as I went to work and he returned from the outdoor vegetable market. The gelato man quickly discerned my plan to try every flavor in his shop and began helping me make each new selection. Obviously, the more proficient one can become in the local language, the more enriching these kinds of experiences will be. However, with good will, you can make a strong human connection, despite language barriers.

It was refreshing to cast off my usual tourist's urgency of purpose and feel that I could simply absorb a bit of Florence's magnificence through daily routine. Depending on how I routed my walk to and from work, I could pass any number of exquisite Florentine sites, lingering on the way home to my heart's content. In this way, I made not the one tourist's stop at Santa Croce, but several visits. On numerous occasions, I was able to study Ghiberti's Gates of Paradise in solitude because I walked through Florence's main square before any tourists were out. I had time to discuss a site or a design detail with others, read more about it, then go back for a second, or even a fifth look.

Settling down to work in a foreign city also means that you can commit to extended experiences, such as a cookery course. In Florence, the Italian cooking class was a wonderful vehicle for informal faculty-student interaction and great fun for everyone. At each session, we cooked an entire meal, and then sat down to eat it. The wine started flowing after the food was far enough along to ensure a meal that evening. I remain scarred by Chef Massimo's emotional denunciation of my gnocchi dough, but life goes on.

My residence in Ireland conjures up very different, but equally marvelous memories. The opportunity to live on the historic and sheltering campus of Trinity College was an unforgettable experience. On almost any day of the week I could watch a cricket game from my window or pay homage to the Book of Kells, located just a few cobblestones away. Theater in the home of Becket and Wilde is as memorable as the morning smell of the day's batch of brewing Guinness stout. By having a front row seat on the Northern Ireland news, I gained entirely new insights on the peace efforts and learned of the unstinting gratitude of the Irish for President Clinton's efforts to help end the historic "troubles" of that small island. And yes, practically everyone in Ireland *is* friendly and welcoming and ready to tell an entertaining story over a pint of beer. The sociability of that culture is something to behold.

Abandoning our routine lives to live and work abroad takes planning and flexibility. Trying to get a job done in an unfamiliar setting can be frustrating and draining. Are the hassles worth it? My answer is absolutely, unequivocally, yes! For me, the rewards of living abroad and immersing into another culture far outweigh the difficulties. There is no better way to know another place, and there is no better means of gaining a personal perspective on our work and on our lives. Best of all, this is adventure!

Retiring Around the World

Muriel Efron

SUMMARY. This article is about the author's temporary work in three different foreign locations–Australia, Israel, and Bermuda. She tells how she found the positions, what it was like to live and work in each place, and gives advice on how to find such positions. She ends with a list of law library associations, their listserves, and how to contact them. *[Article copies available for a fee from The Haworth Document Delivery Service: 1-800-342-9678. E-mail address: <getinfo@haworthpressinc.com> Website: <http://www.HaworthPress.com> © 2000 by The Haworth Press, Inc. All rights reserved.]*

Do you want to travel, see distant places and earn money at the same time? This is one librarian's story of doing just that. There are many different ways to find work abroad. This is my story–how I managed to live and work in Australia, Israel, and Bermuda. I will tell you of my experiences, followed by some advice on how to do it. There are several components to overseas work, including finding an opening, applying for it, finding a place to live when you go there, and, of course, doing the work and exploring the area once you are there.

Since I first learned about Australia as a school child in Philadelphia, when we debated whether Australia was the largest island or the smallest continent, I had wanted to travel there. As I learned more about that far-off place, I realized it would take more than the usual two week vacation to see as much of it as I wanted to see. So through

---

Muriel Efron is Part-Time Law Library Consultant, Greenberg Traurig, West Palm Beach, FL.

[Haworth co-indexing entry note]: "Retiring Around the World." Efron, Muriel. Co-published simultaneously in *Legal Reference Services Quarterly* (The Haworth Information Press, an imprint of The Haworth Press, Inc.) Vol. 18, No. 3, 2000, pp. 25-33; and: *Law Librarians Abroad* (ed: Janet Sinder) The Haworth Information Press, an imprint of The Haworth Press, Inc., 2000, pp. 25-33. Single or multiple copies of this article are available for a fee from The Haworth Document Delivery Service [1-800-342-9678, 9:00 a.m. - 5:00 p.m. (EST). E-mail address: getinfo@haworthpressinc.com].

my child-rearing and working years, it was a distant dream. Then my daughter said that instead of just dreaming and yearning about going to Australia, I should think of a practical way to get there.

I was near retirement age, but wanted to continue to work, as I enjoy being a law librarian. My dilemma–how could I go to Australia for an extended period of time and continue to earn money? The obvious answer was to live and work in Australia. I didn't know anyone in Australia, but I knew how to find colleagues there. I looked in the AALL directory, and wrote letters to every Australian law librarian listed in it. I briefly gave my credentials, explained that I was interested in temporary work, and would welcome any advice anyone could give me.

Several librarians wrote that they would keep me in mind and suggested joining the Australian Association of Law Librarians Group to receive their newsletter, which would list openings. About a month later, I received a telephone call from Lynn Pollack, then the director of the Law Courts Library in Sydney. Her library had a grant for a temporary position for a librarian to install and teach legal CD-ROMs to their patrons–the solicitors, barristers, judges, and other law librarians who used their library. They were purchasing American and Australian CD-ROMs, and she needed someone who was familiar with this medium.

I sent Lynn my resume, and she offered me the position, after doing the necessary searching for an Australian. There were qualified law librarians in Australia, but they were working full time. It was my good fortune that no-one there wanted the temporary position. I was able to obtain a work visa by contacting the Australian embassy and by doing the necessary paper work. (Every country has its complicated procedures!)

I retired at the end of September, 1990, and was in Sydney by Friday, October 12th–less than two weeks later. The library had reserved a room for me at the YWCA, which was within walking distance from the Law Courts building. I landed at 6 a.m., was at the Y by 8 a.m., and was too energized to think of sleeping. I couldn't get into my room anyway, so I stored the luggage and walked over to the library. I still remember the initial thrill and excitement. I was actually in Australia, walking in Sydney and seeing the places I had looked at on the city map. I met Lynn and Josie Taylor, the assistant director, and other staff members, all of whom immediately made me feel right at home. They had an extensive collection of American law books, which made me feel even more at home.

By Monday afternoon, through contacts the library had arranged for me, I had found a wonderful efficiency apartment on the North Shore, overlooking the magnificent Sydney harbor with a breathtaking view of the opera house. How lucky could one person be!

The first week, I established a bank account, put gas, electric, and telephone service in my name, and found a grocery store that would deliver. I didn't want to rent a car, as I didn't quite trust myself to drive on the left side of the road. I had enough to do learning to look carefully both ways before crossing any streets!

For the next three months, I worked at the Law Courts Library. We had several stations set up for using CD-ROMs. I set up daily schedules to teach the use of the CD-ROMs to library patrons. Both the state and federal judges were interested in learning how to do the research themselves. We even had a portable station that I could take to judges' chambers to give them private instruction. They were fascinated with the (then) new technology. We had CD-ROMs for case law in a few of the Australian states, including New South Wales and Tasmania. In addition to the judges, I taught the barristers and solicitors who used the library. We also had law librarians from other libraries who came in to use the library and wanted to learn about CD-ROMs. I kept records on everything I did, e.g., the people I trained each day, the CDs they were most interested in, and the time involved. I also worked on preparing a detailed booklet with specific instructions for using each of the different CDs we had in the library and did specific research for patrons when requested.

When there was free time, I showed the library staff the intricacies of using the *United States Code* and the *Code of Federal Regulations*. They did not have the separate distinctions of statutory and administrative law that we do in the U.S., so were happy to have hands-on instruction. (This was before this information was available online.) In turn, I learned about British and Australian law.

I also had the opportunity to go to a meeting of law librarians in New South Wales, and enjoyed meeting my Australian colleagues. Every morning, I took a fifteen-minute ferry ride to Circular Quay, then either walked 5 blocks or took the bus to the courthouse. In Sydney, the New South Wales State Court and the Federal Court are in the same building, hence the Law Courts Library serves both state and federal courts. Since the library is in the heart of downtown, I did sightseeing on lunch hours, as well as shopping in the large department stores nearby.

On the weekends, I did the usual tourist things as well as taking trains and busses to all parts of town just to explore. One of my favorite places was Bondi Beach, which looks just like its pictures–a vast semicircle with beautiful white sand and bathers galore.

I went to the wine country, saw the Blue Mountains, spent a full day visiting Canberra, the national capital. I went to the museums, the libraries, and the magnificent Botanical Gardens which are near the Opera House. Of course, I also went to several productions at the famous Opera House. People were very friendly, and if it were not so very far from home, I could be very happy living there.

I worked until the end of the year, joining in their Christmas festivities and enjoying my newfound friends. I did miss Thanksgiving! That is a uniquely American holiday. I saved enough money to travel for six weeks before going home. A good friend came over from the U.S. to visit and traveled with me for three weeks. We went to Tasmania, the island state of Australia, not usually included in general tours of Australia, and found it to be thoroughly delightful. There we rented a car and drove from Launceston to Hobart; that is, from one end of the island to the other. If you head south from Hobart, the next stop is Antarctica! Tasmania is similar to New Zealand, with its magnificent mountains, its large sheep population, and its very British atmosphere.

We spent time in Melbourne, also a delightful city, and took a day trip to Phillips Island to see the fairy penguins that come ashore every day at twilight with food for their baby penguins who are hiding in the hillside. It is an incredible sight, as you cannot imagine how each parent penguin knows its own baby. They pass crying little penguins begging for food until they get to their own offspring and put the food carried from the ocean into their little mouths.

When we returned to Sydney, my friend helped me close up my apartment with its unforgettable view of the Sydney harbor and Opera House, and then she had to go back to the U.S. I toured for another three weeks. I took the train from Sydney to Perth and experienced the vastness of the country. I visited law libraries in Perth and saw people I had met via e-mail while working in Sydney. I also took the Ghan train to Alice Springs, took a sunrise flight over Ayres Rock, and enjoyed seeing the Outback I had heard so much about. I also visited

Adelaide on the way back to Sydney, another enchanting city well worth a more extended visit.

My experience in Australia whetted my appetite for more foreign work. On a visit to Israel to visit my son and his family, I visited law libraries in that country. From one of the law librarians in Jerusalem, I learned that a new law school was going to open at Haifa University near the town where my son lives.

I thought working there would be ideal for me. I could see my children, tour the country, and earn money at the same time. I sent my resume to the library director asking about temporary work in the law library and found out that the law collection was to be housed in the regular university library. They were not going to have a separate law library as we do in the U.S.

The library director did not have anyone on his staff trained in the law. When he found out I had experience in British law from working in Australia, as well as knowledge of American law, he wanted me to start work the day after I met him! A law library consultant had recommended what to buy, but they needed someone to help with cataloging the collection and to provide reference service, as well as recommend adding to the basic collection. Since Israel was once a British mandate and still was largely governed by British law, my Australian experience was invaluable. They also relied heavily on American law, and, of course, I knew that well.

Living quarters were not a problem here, as my son helped me find a small apartment near his home. Every day I rode a bus along the Mediterranean coast to the central bus station, then took another bus up, up the hills to the University, which is on the top of Mount Carmel, with a majestic view of Haifa harbor.

The law collection included Israeli laws and cases, as well as basic legal collections of British and American law. My job was to get it organized, see that material was catalogued, suggest new material, show the other librarians how to use the English material, and work with the serials people on loose-leaf services. I didn't know Hebrew, which was a handicap, but since everyone else spoke English, I managed.

In Haifa, too, I learned as much as I taught. Because Israel is such a small country, there is a great deal of international legal work. The law students had to become familiar with the legal systems of other common law countries, as well as European and Arabic law. We had materials in English, German, Arabic, and French. I found them more advanced technologically at that point than many places in the U.S. By necessity, they had to have electronic access to as much material as possible.

It was a fascinating mix of students, and I saw Israeli, Arab, and Jewish students studying together every day. Also, it was the busiest library I have ever worked in. There were banks of computer stations for the online catalog, and there were usually two or three students waiting to use each terminal. These were also the most dedicated and hard working students I have ever worked with.

Although there were law librarians at the other law schools in Israel–Jerusalem, Tel Aviv, and Bar Ilan Universities–there were no trained law librarians in Haifa. So I helped to train their reference librarians on the use of the legal collection. The University also has a library science school, and I helped teach a student who later became the law librarian. We are still in touch, and just recently she was able to send me an Israeli case a lawyer needed in the U.S.

After these two experiences, I had a taste of working abroad and wanted to do it again. By now, I realized one of the best ways is to be a member of the various law library associations around the world. I joined the British and American Association of Law Libraries (BIALL), and it was in one of their newsletters that I heard of a temporary opening in Bermuda to replace someone on maternity leave.

I e-mailed Karen Skiffington-Simpson at her law firm in Hamilton, Bermuda, and faxed her my resume. Bermuda has very strict laws regarding aliens working there. (Yes, remember, when you are working in a foreign country, you are the alien!) However, there were no Bermudans with the necessary qualifications who were willing to work for just a few months. Again, my Australian and Israeli experiences worked to my advantage, since Bermuda is part of the British Commonwealth, and knowledge of British law was essential.

Working in Bermuda was truly a dream. It is as beautiful as we hear it is, and the people are very friendly. To live there was so much better than just visiting for a week or so. Since it is a small island, only about 26 miles long, and has an excellent transportation system, it is easy to get around.

Rental cars are not available, as they restrict the number of cars on the island in the interest of avoiding traffic congestion. An alternative to having a car is to rent a moped. Riding a moped is only for the young and foolish, in my opinion, especially since they drive on the left side of the road, as in England.

Karen, the librarian whom I was replacing, gave birth to a beautiful little girl baby the day I arrived in Bermuda, so we didn't have our planned overlap. However, she was as close as the telephone, and we were in frequent communication. The firm had found a lovely small apartment for me, right on the ocean and on a bus line. The library assistant, a delightful American woman who had married a Bermudan, was invaluable, and I learned about Bermuda law from her. We would walk over to the courthouse and get copies of all the Bermuda court opinions.

Karen had devised an index to the opinions, which I continued, and other law firms in the country used our index. Again, because we were in a very small country (about 60,000 people), much of the legal work was overseas. Our firm represented many offshore companies, and there was constant demand for online searches, and heavy use of all legal databases. Since our firm did the digest of Bermuda law for Martindale-Hubbell, we were often called on by firms in other countries for assistance in finding Bermuda law. Karen had built an extensive list of contacts in many places, and I made good use of them.

Bermuda is a delightful place. I thoroughly enjoyed living and working there. I went from one end of the island to the other–from the Dockyard area in the western end to St. George on the eastern end. I visited the aquarium, the Perfumaria with its beautiful flower gardens, and the many historical forts still standing. I walked many parts of the old Railroad Trail. I had tea in the finest hotels in Bermuda and ate in many of their great restaurants. As in the other places where I worked, I felt very much at home and made many friends with whom I am still in touch. (E-mail is the greatest invention since sliced bread!)

When I returned from Bermuda, I had the opportunity to work part-time here at home for the law firm from which I retired when I went to Australia. I am enjoying that so much that I am not looking for other overseas work experiences now, but I do stay on the overseas listserves! One never knows what will come up!

Here is some advice for those of you who want to do this. First of all, you must be flexible. You have to be willing to live differently than you do at home, do without a car if necessary, learn about other currency, and be homesick at times. You have to consider finding a place to live, means of transportation, cleaners, beauty shops, doctors, dentists, and bank accounts among other things. You must have health insurance.

If you are interested in working abroad, update your resume, subscribe to overseas listserves, and join other law library associations to receive their publications. It was through the BIALL Newsletter that I heard of the opening in Bermuda. Even if you do not join, sign on to their listserves, where you also will see openings for positions. Be proactive. If you want to work in a particular place, contact all the law libraries you can find via directories or the Internet and let them know you are interested in working there. That is how I found the Australian position. If you vacation abroad, contact law libraries and arrange to visit them while you are there. That is how I found out about the Israeli position.

At the end of this article is a list of some law library associations you may want to join, with information about their Web sites, listserves, and contacts.

I urge anyone who wants to work and travel abroad to take advantage of any opportunity that comes along, or that you can create for yourself. My life has been enriched by my experiences, and I feel very fortunate to have been able to combine my love of travel with my love of my profession.

SELECTIVE LIST OF LAW LIBRARY ASSOCIATIONS

Australian Law Librarians Group (ALLG)
Contact: Mary Greenfield, National Convenor
e-mail: mary.greenfield@butterworths. com.au
To subscribe to listserve e-mail: majordomo@uow.edu.au
In message say: subscribe anz-law-librarians-one [your name]
Web site: http://www.allg.asn.au

British and Irish Association of Law Libraries (BIALL)
Contact: Mrs. Susan Frost
BIALL Administrator; 26 Myton Crescent; Warwick CV34 6QA DX: 11884
Leamington Spa; Tel/fax: 01926 491717
e-mail: susanfrost@compuserve.com
To subscribe to listserve: e-mail: mailbase@mailbase.ac.uk
In message say: Ajoin lis-law [your name]
Web site: http://www.biall.org.uk

Canadian Association of Law Libraries (CALL)
Contact: CALL National Office; PO Box 1570, 4 Cataraqui St. Suite 310, Kingston, Ont. K7L 5C8.

Administrative officer: Elizabeth Hooper, e-mail: call@adan.kingston.net
To subscribe to listserve: e-mail: call-1-server@unb.ca
In message say: subscribe call-1 [your name]
example: subscribe call-l Wayne Gretzky (this example is from their Web site!)
Web site: http://www.callacbd.ca

New Zealand Law Librarian's Group (NZLLG)
Contact: The Treasurer NZ Law Librarian's Group, Inc. PO Box 2438, Wellington Central, New Zealand; or Robin Anderson, National Convenor,
e-mail: library@wdis.org.nz
To subscribe to listserve: e-mail: majordomo@vuw.ac.nz
In message say: subscribe law-lib [your email address]
Messages to the group should be posted to: law-lib@vuw.ac.nz
Web site: http://www.knowledge-basket.co.nz/nzllg

Organization of South African Law Libraries (OSALL)
Contact: Ms. Elizabeth Bourne, Treasurer, OSALL, PO Box 785812. Sandton, 2146; South Africa. E-mail: Ebourne@bowman.co.za
To subscribe to listserve: e-mail Majordomo@sunsite.wits.ac.za
In message say: subscribe osall [your email address]
Web site: http://sunsite.wits.ac.za/osall

Developing Law Library Resources in Eritrea

Thomas R. French

SUMMARY. This article discusses the author's experiences in helping to develop and revitalize the law school and law library collections in the East African nation of Eritrea. This project was part of a rebuilding effort following a thirty year struggle for independence from Ethiopia in which much of Eritrea's infrastructure and public institutions were destroyed. Among the pressing issues presented to the author were funding, collection development, space-planning, staffing and services needs. *[Article copies available for a fee from The Haworth Document Delivery Service: 1-800-342-9678. E-mail address: <getinfo@haworthpressinc.com> Website: <http://www.HaworthPress.com> © 2000 by The Haworth Press, Inc. All rights reserved.]*

INTRODUCTION

The East African State of Eritrea formally declared its independence in 1993 following a thirty-year war of secession from Ethiopia. Eritrea is located on the Red Sea south and east of Sudan, north of Ethiopia, and across the water from Saudi Arabia. Asmara is its capital city.

Since 1994, I have had the opportunity to travel to Eritrea three

---

Thomas R. French is Director of the Law Library and Associate Professor of Law, Syracuse University.

This article is based on a talk given at the 1997 Annual Meeting of the American Association of Law Libraries.

[Haworth co-indexing entry note]: "Developing Law Library Resources in Eritrea." French, Thomas R. Co-published simultaneously in *Legal Reference Services Quarterly* (The Haworth Information Press, an imprint of The Haworth Press, Inc.) Vol. 18, No. 3, 2000, pp. 35-48; and: *Law Librarians Abroad* (ed: Janet Sinder) The Haworth Information Press, an imprint of The Haworth Press, Inc., 2000, pp. 35-48. Single or multiple copies of this article are available for a fee from The Haworth Document Delivery Service [1-800-342-9678, 9:00 a.m. - 5:00 p.m. (EST). E-mail address: getinfo@haworthpressinc.com].

times to conduct a library needs assessment, set up a law reading room at the University of Asmara, and to work on ongoing collection development projects at the University and the Eritrean Ministry of Justice. These projects have mostly been funded by the United States Information Agency, the United States Agency for International Development, the American Bar Association, and the University of North Carolina.[1] I first became involved with these projects as part of my work at the University of North Carolina Law Library.

The purpose of this article is to describe how I became a participant in the project, what I did, what I learned, and to make a few suggestions for those who may be interested in this type of activity.

SOME BACKGROUND

Over the past century, Eritrea has been an Italian Colony (1890s-1941) under British administration (1941-52) and federated with Ethiopia (1952-91). It has a land area approximately the size of Pennsylvania, with a population of 3 to 4 million. There are at least 9 distinct ethnic groups in the country with their own languages and cultures. The population is roughly half Muslim and half Christian. Arabic and Tigrinya are its official working languages, although English is the language of instruction starting in junior high school through university.[2]

In April 1994, Dr. Wolde'ab, the President of the University of Asmara, visited Chapel Hill to discuss a linkage with the University of North Carolina and North Carolina Central University. The purpose of the linkage, which included plans for faculty participation from political science, journalism, public policy, and law, was to help improve the University of Asmara's overall capacity to train its students to take leading roles in the development of Eritrea. Funding was available to provide support to the University to educate Eritreans in the rule of law and to promote democratic values.[3] Dr. Wolde'ab proposed that faculty from Chapel Hill and elsewhere would travel to Asmara to conduct needs assessments, act as consultants in curriculum development, and provide temporary faculty and other support as needed. I was invited to attend a meeting with Dr. Wolde'ab as one of the representatives from the law faculty. Three months later, North Carolina's University Center for International Studies asked if I could leave for Eritrea within the week to conduct a needs assessment involving the law program there. Five days later, I left for Asmara.

THE FIRST VISIT

Upon arriving in Asmara, I attended a meeting with the President of the University, who outlined his goals for the North Carolina-Asmara linkage and how my visit could contribute to the program. He wanted to improve the law department, and possibly, as the law faculty was eager to do, even upgrade it from an undergraduate diploma course to a full LL.B. program.[4] He expected me to work with the law faculty to make suggestions as to what would be needed to accomplish this. The next day I met with the Eritrean Minister of Justice, who elaborated on her needs for addressing the critical shortage of "qualified" legal workers in all levels of the justice system from judges on the High Court to District Court personnel.

From the Ministry of Justice, I was sent to the Constitutional Commission, the committee created to draft a constitution for the country.[5] As part of its work, the Commission also conducted civic education programs and held seminars on constitutional issues throughout the country and in cities abroad where there were large numbers of Eritrean expatriates.[6]

The following day I was back at the Ministry of Justice, where I spent several hours with the legal advisor to the Minister of Justice, who talked to me about the Ethiopian Civil and Criminal Codes which Eritrea had inherited from Ethiopia. He then told me about his work in drafting a new civil code for Eritrea by modifying the Ethiopian code and about the country's need for "trained legal workers" at all levels of the government. After this meeting, the legal advisor presented me with a wish list of legal materials that he felt would be useful in his work. The list consisted mostly of European codes and some U.S. materials, such as hornbooks, *Black's Law Dictionary*, and law reviews.

On the fourth day of my visit, I had the opportunity to meet with the law faculty at the University of Asmara. At this meeting, also attended by a legal advisor from the Ministry of Justice, the law faculty briefed me about their program and its need for additional staff,[7] resources, books, journals, and equipment. During the meeting, I became aware of some disagreement between the law department and Ministry of

Justice centered on the conflicting needs and goals of the ministry and the law department. The Ministry of Justice wanted a short-term expedited program of legal education to meet the immediate needs of the justice system, or, in their words, to "train legal workers." I understood "legal workers" to mean all types of personnel, including agency staff, court clerks, lawyers, and judges. The law faculty wanted a more long-term degree program emphasizing the development of lawyers, with the training of "legal workers" being a secondary objective.

A law library was on the minds of both the faculty and the ministry, but they disagreed on the general nature and location of such a facility. Justice wanted it to be practitioner-oriented and located in the Ministry of Justice. The law faculty were thinking more along the lines of a research center to be located at the University. They all agreed that the country did not currently have the resources needed for two libraries, although both sides acknowledged a pressing need to upgrade standards and knowledge of the law throughout the country.

During the next week, I met several more times with the law faculty and at the Ministry of Justice to gather information and work on the issues that had been raised during my first week. I spent time scrutinizing the law collections at the Public Library (which was a USIA sponsored operation) the British Council Library), and the Ministry of Education Library to ascertain what types of legal materials they housed. Unfortunately, the law collections in these libraries had little to offer. I also had the opportunity to meet with the University Librarian, who invited me to attend a University Library committee meeting. From the librarian and by attending the committee meeting, I learned of the dire need of the University for books, journals, staff training, and equipment. One of the library's goals was to have one copy of the course textbooks for every two students in each class. Another was to subscribe to five journals for each academic department–most journal subscriptions having been canceled in 1989 due to war-related circumstances.

I spent the following few days writing up a report and presenting it to the law faculty and the Ministry of Justice. In it, I reviewed the issues and problems raised during my discussions and my interpretations of them. Eritrea needed skilled and knowledgeable workers for the administration of justice, including court personnel, judges, lawyers, legal workers, and law faculty. Everyone desired a respectable law school and law library collection. Cost effectiveness and the wise use of available resources were underlying concerns. Reaching consensus on exactly how these goals were to be reached was problematic. Areas of disagreement included the nature and location of the law library/legal research facility, exact equipment and collection development needs, how to improve the law curriculum, and how best to meet the training needs of faculty, staff, and legal workers.

Everyone agreed that funding was needed to establish a law library, to begin staff development programs, to develop a records management system for the courts, to provide educational materials, to establish a legal aid clinic, and, in the words of the Ministry of Justice, to provide "funding to create programs aimed at solving the problems created by the shortage of qualified lawyers in Eritrea." How great a shortage? In 1994, Kentucky, with about the same population as Eritrea, had about 10,000 or 11,000 attorneys, while Eritrea had fewer than 100.

Without really knowing much about the situation in Eritrea, much less understanding it, I made several suggestions in hopes that those responsible for resolving the issues could work out their differences. For the library, thinking along the lines of an academic library system in the United States with a main library and several branches, I split the baby.

I suggested that the University library and law department be responsible for all acquisitions and processing, with the University having responsibility for storing lesser-used materials. I proposed that both the University and the Ministry should have their own sets of standard reference works, along with the most necessary and most likely to be used sources. I proposed that the University should have responsibility for creating a comprehensive collection, including the more research-oriented materials in addition to the texts and other materials needed for curriculum support. I recommended that the University begin a staff development program in the library to familiarize library staff with some of the unique characteristics of legal publishing.

In any event, I argued that there should be liberal sharing of resources between the two institutions, some type of union list or shared catalog created, and, of course, provision for a document delivery service. The most needed resources were Ethiopian legal materials, including the *Journal of Ethiopian Law*, of which I discovered that no one had a complete set. Knowing that there was funding available for equipment as well as books, I suggested CD-ROM and microfiche formats whenever possible to cut down on the cost of shipping. At the time, in 1994, the Internet was not quite as important as it is today, and e-mail was only rumored to be available through Healthnet at the Ministry of Health. In any event, I was told by everyone that it would be at least ten years before it would be financially or technologically feasible for either.[8]

I spent the rest of my time on this trip talking to the law faculty to develop lists of teaching materials, texts, and treatises they needed for their program and which I would arrange for them to purchase upon my return to the United States. For their part, they agreed to consider my report and decide where to go from there.

THE SECOND VISIT

A year later, I was invited back to "set up the law library" at the University. I was also asked to talk more about CD-ROMs, which, thanks to Kathie Price and New York University, were beginning to arrive, though they were not readily available for anyone to use at the time.

This second trip was much more challenging in several ways. Rather than being asked to listen to the needs of the law faculty, take notes, and make general suggestions, I was expected to answer very specific and sometimes difficult questions, such as how many computers and what types of modems they would need. They wanted technical suggestions, even asking what computers I would recommend for some of the faculty to buy for their own use. Of course, I also had to work on the stated purpose of the trip, to establish a law library–a project that had to be finished in just a few weeks.

The University provided me with an apartment in a building housing foreign faculty. This afforded me the opportunity to live on the economy rather than being taken care of in a hotel. It presented several interesting challenges, not the least of which were shopping in local markets and cooking on a two-burner propane stove–no fast food or microwave oven here. It also gave me the opportunity to live, briefly, with people from several countries, including Sudan, Uganda, Canada, India, and Britain. Living in this apartment house was one of the best parts of my whole experience in Eritrea, because I was able to see what it is like to live in a faraway, culturally different place.

Back at the University, I quickly discovered that what the faculty and I thought I was going to do was not necessarily what the University President expected me to do. When I arrived, the law faculty and I were under the impression that I was to set up a law library separate from the University Library. The law library was to consist of the law collection, then housed in the University Library, and recently donated books from New York University, the D.C. Bar Association, the A.B.A., the University of North Carolina, and various other donors.

The President, however, made it clear to all of us that the decision to create such a library had not been made. In fact, he was opposed to the idea, fearing that it would establish a precedent so that all of the other faculties in the University would demand their own libraries. Instead, he wanted me to work with the University Librarian to see if the law faculty's concerns could be taken care of within the University Library. These concerns included complaints about restricted access within the library: special written permission was required every time a student wanted to use the reference library where all of the journals and the bulk of the Ethiopian legal materials were shelved. While the library itself was open until 10:00 p.m., the reference library closed at 5:00. Compounding the problem was general overcrowding in the library, which made working there extremely difficult and uncomfortable for patrons.

Many on the law faculty felt that the bureaucratic nature of the library inhibited the faculty from making materials available to students in a timely manner. This was especially evident in that it sometimes took weeks to have items placed on reserve. For a faculty member who wanted materials available the next day, this time frame was completely unacceptable. Not surprisingly, the faculty assumed that if they had control over a law library this would not happen.

Another complication was that the library's legal materials were scattered in several areas throughout the library, making it even more difficult for students to utilize them. To make matters worse, because of other demands on the library's time, hundreds of books, both donated and others purchased by the University, that were in storage when I visited the year before, were still in storage in a warehouse–not yet even up to "backlog" status. Considering the exigencies under which the university library operated, this situation, while frustrating for faculty, was also understandable.

The president told me to meet with the librarian and try to work all of this out. The librarian was cordial and wanted to be cooperative but, understandably, was very concerned that creating a special law library would negatively impact the University library's ability to account for resources and control circulation. As a librarian, I sympathized with him, especially when he stated that he was fearful that the creation of what was now downsized from a law library to a law reading room would endanger the few legal resources that the library did have by removing them from the librarian's control and putting them under the control of the law faculty. One other small problem surfaced: no one had thought about where this new law reading room was to be located.

I reported these concerns to the President, who told me to study the issues and report back to him the next week with recommendations for solving them. After prolonged negotiations, the library and the law faculty agreed that a separate reading room for law would be created under the jurisdiction of the law faculty. Finding an appropriate space for a reading room was the next issue to be resolved. One possible location, proposed by the librarian, was the English Department's "underutilized" reading room. The faculty liked this proposal, and we went to visit the English reading room. It turned out to be a classroom-sized space used primarily for storing multiple copies of English texts, a language lab, and who knows what from the now defunct French Department. The library and law faculty determined that this would be an acceptable location provided that additional shelving was installed, the French materials were removed, and the Dean of Arts and Sciences agreed to it.

The Dean was willing to give up the space. He instructed me to throw away the French materials and set up a law library in the room. The University promised to have shelving delivered right away, and I began to think about how to get the books moved from the library and warehouse and to work out a floor plan and shelf arrangement. At this point, the University's Vice President for Business stopped in to tell me that the shelving could not be delivered before I was to return to the U.S. so I should go ahead and get rid of the French language materials and shift and compact the English materials to free up space on the existing shelves for the law materials.

Unfortunately, no one bothered to consult with the chair of the English department or its faculty, who soon learned of what I was doing and, to put it mildly, were not thrilled with the idea. For the next couple of days, no one knew for sure if there would be a law reading room. After still another meeting with the President, law faculty, University Librarian, and the English Department chair, I was instructed to get on with the project. I cleaned out the space in the room, moved furniture, packed up boxes of French language materials, and inventoried the law materials that were to be moved into the space now labeled "Room 300" so as not to rekindle any jurisdictional disputes.

Plans in hand for the move, I approached the law faculty and asked for permission to ask for student volunteers to help move materials to the reading room and then to set them up on the shelves. By this time, rumors were circulating among the law students that they were about to get their own library. Anticipation was high, and when I asked the class to volunteer, everyone did. For those who have moved libraries, you know that actually getting the books from points A, B, and C to point D is not an especially easy task. Now think of moving those books with no book trucks, hand carts, or other equipment with wheels and think about moving those books from the second floor of a building across a courtyard to the third floor of a building with no elevator. Add to this the fact that the movers were all volunteer law students and that the move was scheduled for a Saturday morning after their last class for the week was over, and you might be as astounded as I was to see that all of the students actually showed up for the move. The faculty, including a visiting Fulbright Professor from the U.S., did too.

In a few hours' time, we managed to move the books, clean them, and arrange them on the shelves. After that, I took everyone out for refreshments at a popular student hangout near the University, and the law department had the beginnings of a library containing sections for U.S., Ethiopian/Eritrean, Italian, European, international, and refugee law. The United States section contains *American Jurisprudence 2d*, *American Law Reports*, the *United States Code Service*, New York statutes, the *Code of Federal Regulations*, dozens of case books, the *Supreme Court Reporter*, a fairly complete set of Nutshells, and several hornbooks.

This was a rewarding project in many ways. Being able to observe the enthusiasm of the faculty and students and their willingness to work to improve their situation was inspiring. Participating in the project also allowed me to make a small contribution to a new and struggling law school and required me to use most everything I've learned in over twenty years as a librarian in terms of planning and working with people and materials and mediating the needs of users and available resources. I also came to realize that, although many of the issues and concerns facing libraries, faculty, and students in Eritrea may be similar to those in the United States, the solutions to these problems and concerns may be very different.

THIRD VISIT

My third trip to Asmara, during the summer of 1996, came about after the Ministry of Justice heard about the law reading room project at the University. By now, some of the issues between the law faculty and the Ministry of Justice had been worked out, and USAID was funding a book purchase program for the Ministry of Justice. Because of the contacts I had made at the Ministry of Justice during my previous trips, I was invited to return to work with them in determining their needs and then to work with USAID in actually acquiring the books. While I was in Eritrea on this trip, I spent most of my time talking to the legal staff in the Ministry to ascertain their needs. We discussed subject areas that they were interested in, including legal ethics, jurisprudence, law office management, comparative law, labor, contracts, insurance, civil law systems, including codes, Islamic law, judicial administration, legal writing in civil law countries, drafting, dictionaries, form books, and historical commentaries on law and legal subjects. For American law, they wanted books on constitutional law, ethics, banking, evidence, tax, environmental law, and mediation and arbitration.

From these discussions, and with the help of several publishers' catalogs that I had brought with me, I created lists of possible titles for their approval. After we formulated a list of about 500 approved titles, we began the process of purchasing them by seeking bids from various vendors in the United States. Yankee Book Peddler and Hein were especially helpful in acquiring these titles. They deserve thanks and credit for their patience and willingness to adjust their own procedures to accommodate the needs of the Eritrean legal community, and, at the same time, satisfying the many bookkeeping and auditing requirements of the United States government and the State of North Carolina.

While my official involvement in these projects ended three years ago, from time to time I get requests for additional materials or advice from the people I worked with in Eritrea. As such, these projects are continuing, and once in a while new ones emerge. Law faculty in Asmara contact me when they need a specific resource for a project they are working on, and, as additional funding comes available for new materials and resources, I am often asked to provide some new assistance.

SUGGESTIONS FOR OTHERS

What are my suggestions for others who may participate in the ABA or similar programs? Try to learn as much about where you are going as you can before you leave. I was pretty ill-prepared for my first trip, having had only five days notice, but by the second I knew a little bit about the country and its history. Learn to roll with the punches and have a sense of humor. There are bound to be misunderstandings. Whatever you do, do not assume you have all of the answers. One of the major lessons I took away from my experience in Eritrea is that sometimes there are no answers to questions raised. What you think you are going to do may not be exactly what you will be doing once you get there.

Be flexible and resourceful. Projects such as the ones I have been involved with are not for people who cannot deal with ambiguity. Be on the look out for projects you can do in addition to whatever your main purpose is. Be prepared to do some staff development while you are there. Use every bit of extra time you have to learn about the library or law school you are visiting. Take the time to peruse the library, learn their collections, get to know the staff–it will make your time there all the more beneficial. But if you can't live without all of the conveniences and comforts of home, or even some of them, don't go.

Travel lightly. There are laundries for your clothes–use the extra space in your luggage for books to give away. Take the one thing you can't live without–in my case peanut butter–and a cheap short wave radio, especially if you are going to a country where whatever languages you know are not widely spoken. Be as charming as you can possibly be. If you like the people you are working with and they like you, the whole experience will be more rewarding both to you and the institution you are visiting.

Try to collect whatever legal publications you can get your hands on to bring back to your library. It wasn't until my second trip that I realized that valuable and unique materials, from the draft constitution to proclamations from the Ministry of Justice, were available for a song at local shops. Now, at a cost of about $10.00, UNC has a pretty rare collection of Eritrean laws from their first five years of independence.[9] Don't think that after you return to the U.S. your work is finished. After your visit to a place such as Asmara, you will be one contact that librarians and faculty in your host country will have in the United States. All kinds of requests for information and help may follow the official end of your project. During the time since my last trip to Asmara, I have been asked to find materials ranging from Eritrean colonial era treaties to the Rome Statute on the International Criminal Court and books to be used by faculty in courses ranging from banking to intellectual property.

HOW TO GET INVOLVED

I was fortunate in that my University had an ongoing project with Asmara and needed a law librarian to participate. When the time came, I was available. There are other ways to become involved beyond having the opportunity fall into your lap. The American Bar Association is one good source. The African Law Initiative[10] sponsors linkages between African and U.S. law schools. Other programs affiliated with the ABA include the Central and East European Law Initiative's Sister Law School Program[11] and The Deans' Committee for Foreign Initiatives.

Let your law school dean know that you are interested in participating in these programs. The World Bank and the United States Agency for International Development[12] have ongoing programs to support the development of democratic institutions in many areas of the world. From time to time, they advertise for librarians to participate in various projects. Don't underestimate the power of word of mouth. I have been asked to participate in projects in Kenya, Uganda, and Lesotho just because someone somewhere knew about my work in Eritrea.

Let people know you are interested in these types of activities. Write about your experiences. Get your name on agencies' lists of potential participants. Apply for Fulbright grants and fellowships. Attend meetings of the Africa Law section of the ABA or the AALS or AALL. Watch law-lib for announcements.[13] There are private sources as well. One that recently advertised for librarians to work in Zimbabwe this summer is the World Library Partnership.[14] Watch the *Federal Register* for announcements of grant proposals, and if your university has an exchange program with another university abroad or has its own program abroad, let their administrators know you would like to participate.

PERSONAL BENEFITS

What did I learn from my experiences in Africa? I learned about a newly developing legal system. I learned that there are not always answers to questions. I learned some of my own limitations, when I didn't know the answers to many of the questions that were asked of me. I think most of all I sharpened my negotiation skills and learned to question even more why we do some of the things that we do in our libraries.

I think that I learned to take myself less seriously and to be able to better distinguish those things that actually matter from those that do not. I saw parts of the world that I never really thought much about before and developed an interest in African, comparative, civil, and Roman law–in other words, areas of law that I rarely encountered before my experience in Eritrea. Finally, I had a priceless and amazing opportunity to work closely with dozens of friendly and welcoming colleagues who are in the process of developing a legal system almost from scratch, with an awe-inspiring dedication to their task at hand.

NOTES

1. These projects include the Democracy Project-Eritrea, the African Law Initiative, and the University Development Linkage Program. *See The Democracy Project-Eritrea at* http://metalab.unc/edu/ucis/eritrea/usia.html (last visited Dec. 12, 1999); United States Agency for International Development, *Human Capacity Development Program at* http://usembassy.state.gov/posts/et9/wwwhd01c. html (last visited Apr. 12, 2000), describing and reporting on the projects in Eritrea.

2. *See generally* Thomas R. French, *Legal Literature of Eritrea: A Bibliographic Essay*, 24 N.C.J.Int'l & Com. Reg. 417 (1999) (Listing citations to published materials concerning the legal and political history and development of Eritrea).

3. *See Democracy Project-Eritrea, supra* note 1.

4. A goal that was reached with the first students receiving their LL.B. degrees in 1998.

5. *See* Bereket Habte Selassie, *Creating a Constitution for Eritrea*, J. Democracy, Apr. 1998.

6. *See generally* Richard A. Rosen, *Constitutional Process, Constitutionalism, and the Eritrean Experience*, 24 N.C.J.Int'l. & Com. Reg. 265 (1999) (discussing the Constitution-making process in Eritrea).

7. With fewer than four faculty members, faculty were required to teach as many as five courses per semester.

8. Internet services actually became available in less than 10 years, *see An Optimal Eritrean Internet: How to Do an Internet Connection that is Right for Eritreans at* http://www.punchdown.org/rvb/email/intntart0899.html (last modified August, 1999).

9. *See supra* note 2, at 446.

10. African Law Initiative at http://www.abanet.org/legaled/ african.html (last visited Dec. 13, 1999).

11. American Bar Association, Central and Eastern European Law Initiative *at* http://www.abanet.org/ceeli/home.html (last visited Dec. 13, 1999).

12. U.S. Agency for International Development, Democracy and Governance *at* http://www.info.usaid.gov/democracy (last visited Dec. 13, 1999).

13. *See* Jo Ann Humphreys, *Law Libraries and Legal Institutions in Ghana*, 15 ALL-SIS Newsletter, Spring 1995, at 8.

14. *World Library Partnership, at* http:RTPnet.org/~wlp (last visited Dec. 13, 1999).

The Clearinghouse for Internships and International Personnel Exchanges

David L. McFadden

SUMMARY. The American Association of Law Libraries' Foreign and Comparative Law Special Interest Section's Clearinghouse for Internships and International Personnel Exchanges provides a listing of libraries willing to participate in visits and exchanges. The purposes and functions of the Clearinghouse are discussed. The author's own experience at the University of Glasgow provides an example of the use of the Clearinghouse survey results to successfully plan and participate in a visit. *[Article copies available for a fee from The Haworth Document Delivery Service: 1-800-342-9678. E-mail address: <getinfo@haworthpressinc.com> Website: <http://www.HaworthPress.com> © 2000 by The Haworth Press, Inc. All rights reserved.]*

The American Association of Law Libraries' Foreign and Comparative Law Special Interest Section, through its Clearinghouse for Internships and International Personnel Exchanges Committee, recognizes an increasing need among our members to gain experience in working with foreign legal information sources and to develop personal and professional relationships with law librarians around the world. The Clearinghouse for Internships and International Personnel Exchanges seeks to channel information to interested law librarians on opportunities to visit libraries abroad.

The committee performs its clearinghouse function by maintaining the results of a survey[1] listing libraries that are willing to participate in

David L. McFadden is Senior Reference Librarian, Southwestern University School of Law Library, Los Angeles, CA.

[Haworth co-indexing entry note]: "The Clearinghouse for Internships and International Personnel Exchanges." McFadden, David L. Co-published simultaneously in *Legal Reference Services Quarterly* (The Haworth Information Press, an imprint of The Haworth Press, Inc.) Vol. 18, No. 3, 2000, pp. 49-57; and: *Law Librarians Abroad* (ed: Janet Sinder) The Haworth Information Press, an imprint of The Haworth Press, Inc., 2000, pp. 49-57. Single or multiple copies of this article are available for a fee from The Haworth Document Delivery Service [1-800-342-9678, 9:00 a.m. - 5:00 p.m. (EST). E-mail address: getinfo@haworthpressinc.com].

exchanges and visits. This list has been published in the SIS's newsletter in the past and is now available at the FCIL Website.[2] The Website also includes testimonials of participants. The purpose of the Clearinghouse is to provide contact information. The actual logistical as well as financial arrangements are up to the participants themselves. The Clearinghouse is not a program, it merely directs people to possible places to visit or exchange. In the future, the Clearinghouse's functions may expand to include financial support information, but even then the purpose would not be to give financial support to specific activities, but to provide information about such opportunities.

Exchanges and visits can have a variety of lengths and characteristics. The principal difference between an exchange and a visit, of course, is that an exchange involves two librarians going to each other's institutions. A visit is unilateral. Both can be profitable, but each is suitable to different needs of those involved. Although each exchange is different, at least some of the regular duties of the exchanging librarians can be taken over by the participants, thereby reducing any adverse impact on the libraries. Of course, not all of the work of the librarians will necessarily be performed by the exchange librarians; the slack will have to be taken up by other librarians.

On a visit, the home library will need to treat the librarian's absence like a vacation or leave and fill in as needed. The Clearinghouse survey includes opportunities of different lengths of time, ranging from just a few weeks to six months or a year. Obviously, the longer the stay, the more complicated the situation becomes. Housing, for example, is one issue that is mentioned in the survey and is a factor in a visit or exchange. Longer stays tend to be more suited for exchanges, whereas shorter stays tend to favor visits.

My own experience is one concrete example of how the Clearinghouse service can be used. For two weeks in late October and early November 1995, I was a visiting law librarian at Glasgow University. I first found out about this opportunity from FCIL's Clearinghouse for Internships and International Personnel Exchanges (at times also known as the Clearinghouse for International Placement). I was intrigued by the idea of visiting a foreign country as a law librarian. I often visit local law libraries while on vacation, and this has allowed me to see supreme court and academic law libraries in Hawaii, Nebraska, and other states. I have also visited a number of county law libraries in my home state of California. It seemed natural, therefore, to expand this interest by going to another country.

Seeing the Clearinghouse's list was what inspired me to think about participating in a visit or exchange. As I am a monolingual person who could not be away from his home library for a long period of time, my choice of libraries was limited. This is one of the great advantages of the Clearinghouse; it offers opportunities for experiences for all sorts of time periods and with varying characteristics.

Preparation for a visit or exchange can be crucial to the experience. Once I decided on an English-speaking country and a short-duration visit, I e-mailed the contact person from the FCIL Clearinghouse survey results, Heather Worlledge-Andrew, and proceeded to negotiate the details of my visit. Using e-mail sped up the process and eliminated time zone difficulties. Since the visit was of such a short duration, I was a house guest of Heather and her husband and commuted to work daily from a small 150-year-old farm house south of Glasgow. Other housing arrangements would have been needed for a longer stay, and, in fact, I did stay at University housing for one night prior to leaving Scotland. I also had to consider the clothing needs for even a two week visit by a Californian to Scotland in October and November.

Beyond the housing and clothing, we needed to consider the nature of my work at Glasgow University. This was left very open-ended, and the specifics of my visit are discussed below. Because the legal system was foreign to me, I also prepared for the visit by going to the Los Angeles County Law Library and teaching myself the rudiments of Scottish legal research. Some familiarity with the legal system and research materials was necessary, since I would be working in a reference environment. Obviously, the nature of the work to be performed during the exchange or visit dictates the depth and nature of preparation needed.

On shorter visits, there is not much opportunity to do more than observe. I was able to see a different legal and legal educational system, the library operations, some of the law school, and a few Scottish courts. Scotland has a unique legal system that has borrowed elements from both civil and common law traditions. For example, the civil law concept of delictual liability is used instead of torts. Also, certain treatises have obtained a status equal to cases and statutes.

Scottish legal education is also different from that in the United

States. Students enter law school at the age of 17 or 18 and study for four years for the LL.B., take one year for a Diploma in Legal Practice, and then serve two years as a trainee in a solicitor's office. The post-diploma training period can be a bit shorter for advocates, the Scottish equivalent of barristers. I had "book knowledge" of the Scottish legal and educational systems, but being there, attending a few classes, and talking to professors and students made it more real for me.

The library I visited was organized differently from most law school libraries in the United States and even from many in the United Kingdom (Strathclyde University, also in Glasgow, has a departmental law library run by a university library employee!). Glasgow University's law librarian, Heather Worlledge-Andrew, is actually their only Subject Specialist in Law. At the time of my visit, she also had responsibility for the European Union and the Council of Europe documents. Her responsibilities have expanded even further since then. Instead of being in an independent departmental library, the law materials are housed as just one of the collections in a much larger library. This was quite different for me, as I have worked exclusively in law libraries. It is much more like the work in an academic library in the U.S. than like the experiences in most law libraries. Staffing levels differed as well. Glasgow, as was mentioned above, has only one person specifically assigned to oversee the law collection. Southwestern University School of Law, my home institution, has approximately the same student population as Glasgow (if Glasgow's business law students are included), but had, at the time, 20 full-time equivalent employees, including 8 professional librarians. Of course, many of the services that Southwestern's library has to provide are covered by general library or law school personnel at Glasgow.

Libraries are not, of course, totally different in Scotland. One thing that made me feel at home was Innopac. Both Glasgow University and Southwestern use this online cataloging system from Innovative Interfaces, so I did not even need to learn a different catalog. I was also able to go online from Los Angeles and see some of their holdings before I left California. This made me feel more at home when I got to Scotland. Also, the general layout and workday at the library were similar to my own.

The structure of the visit is determined by the participants. Sometimes the host library has a very specific purpose in mind. For example, they might need help on a cataloging project, or they may want an American to look over their "foreign" law collection. If it is more project-oriented, it may involve just doing your assigned task as in any other job. The host library may be taking advantage of the program to fill a temporary vacancy in a creative way rather than having a local person step in on a short-term basis. There may be a formal program of having the visitor or exchange librarian actually do the work of various staff members on some sort of rotation basis. This "sampler" approach would be particularly good for longer visits and is similar to what some law firms do with summer clerks.

Frankly, I did not plan out all the details of my visit in advance. It was fairly unstructured, and the specifics were left undetermined when I left Los Angeles. This worked out well at Glasgow but may not work in other settings and probably wouldn't be good for a longer visit or exchange. A large portion of my time consisted of observation. I merely watched Heather do her routine daily work. This may seem too passive but can prove very helpful. Some familiar concerns and problems arose, including frustration over acquisitions procedures, book prices, and budgets; dealing with students trying to do first-year legal research problems; and coping with the library and law school bureaucracy and personalities. Since the library was arranged departmentally by subject, I was also able to meet and observe some non-law specialists as well. I was able to see how government documents collections are handled in the United Kingdom both by talking to Heather, since she handles European Union materials, and to the librarian who managed the U.K. documents.

In addition, I helped the first-year law students with their legal research assignments. I did not teach a class but went out in the stacks to assist the students with "treasure hunt" type problems. That was quite an experience for someone whose only exposure to Scottish law prior to arriving was reading a number of articles and a small book and making an afternoon visit to the Los Angeles County Law Library. Despite this, it was still very familiar, and not much different from helping students at Southwestern. That is what is nice about visits and exchanges. Mine taught me that as librarians, many of our skills are transferable to almost any library. True, the specific books and sources are different, but that is not an insurmountable obstacle.

We were feeling our way regarding the Internet at Southwestern at the time of my visit, and it was helpful to see a library that was a bit ahead of us in its use. I got lists of Heather's and the dean of the law school's favorite international law Internet sites. I also helped with a training session. This has helped immensely at my home law library. Just being in another library allows you to see how others do things. This exchange of ideas and practices is very important to visits and exchanges.

The experiences of the host librarian can shape a visit significantly. Since Heather was a relatively new law librarian, only having worked in law for a little over 18 months at the time I visited, I was able to assist her with international law acquisitions and on some specific reference questions. I was also able to give her some insights about Lexis and Westlaw. Although Glasgow University has Lexis, American educational contracts are more favorable to the library and less limited. Heather does network with other law librarians in Scotland, but it was nice for her to have another law librarian there in person. It also helped remind someone from a larger staff what it is like being the only law librarian in a given institution.

Another more delicate aspect of the visit has to do with who is doing the inviting. Is the institution behind the visit? This may have important consequences for the participants. How much time is allowed by the library or other host institution for the host librarian to work with the visitor or exchange librarian? On my own visit, I felt that my host had plenty of time to spend with me. Of course, the visit was of a short duration, which helped in this regard. Also, my visit was announced in the library newsletter, and I was introduced to a number of librarians and others. I felt welcomed by the library. Nonetheless, on at least one occasion, I was introduced as "Heather's American," and I felt as though it were more of a departmental visit or even a personal visit rather than a library visit. These kinds of issues need to be understood and clarified beforehand to avoid any misunderstandings.

My work was not limited exclusively to the confines of the library. By attending a small seminar class on the U.S. Supreme Court, I unofficially "co-taught" the class. I interjected comments, insights, and perspectives. Luckily, I attended a class early in the term, when it focused on the American legal system and how the Supreme Court fits into it, so this was not too difficult. Arising from this was an opportunity to do a more traditionally librarian activity: research instruction for the seminar students who had to research a Supreme Court justice and related case law.

In order to make the most of the experience, going beyond the walls of the host institution is important. In addition to the Glasgow University experience, I visited another Glasgow law school library, the University of Strathclyde, one afternoon, and later saw a solicitors' firm library. On such a short visit, it is impossible to see all that you would like, but seeing the other libraries gave me other Scottish examples to compare with my host institution. Also, I was able to visit a number of different courts in Glasgow, which helped me understand their legal system. This was another example of being able to do something while on a visit that would be awkward to do on a regular work day in Los Angeles. On a visit like mine, the freedom to be able to truly learn and explore is allowed, and perhaps even expected.

On a visit, while most of the emphasis is on the host institution and the type of experience that it will provide for the visitor, there may also be expectations from the home library or institution. The visit need not be just a personally edifying experience; there can and should be benefits to the home library as well. Obviously, the librarian can formally present his or her experiences in a written report or oral presentation. Beyond that, however, librarians will almost certainly change how they approach their work when they return. There also may be specific demands made on the visiting or exchange librarian. I had an assignment from one of our professors at Southwestern who was writing an article on the right to silence and wanted to know the Scottish perspective on this. By having this extra project, I was able to really learn Scottish legal materials by having to use them.

One revelation that I have had on reflecting on this experience is that I could theoretically have seen and done at least some of the same things here in the U.S., but when do we have time to visit other libraries for more than a few hours or set up domestic exchanges? Many of us do not really visit each others' libraries. It is like the person who only visits the local amusement parks and museums when they have out-of-town guests. It may take a trip across the world to learn about practices and experiences that are common to all law librarians.

As has been already stated, the Clearinghouse does not plan, organize, finance, or participate in the visits or exchanges. Instead, it provides information for the use and benefit of librarians looking for opportunities to travel to a foreign country to learn and share law library methods. Many institutions have existing exchange programs, but these are generally restricted to the members of that particular university or law school. Also, over the years, certain librarians have established personal contacts with librarians abroad and use those contacts to informally arrange visits for themselves and others. The purpose of the Clearinghouse is to help those who do not have these sorts of contacts. My law school has no formal exchange or visitor program. The University of Glasgow is not a sister school to Southwestern. There would have been no way for me to know about this opportunity without the Clearinghouse. The mission and purpose of the Clearinghouse is to make more of these opportunities possible for other law librarians.

NOTES

1. *See* Appendix 1, *infra* for a copy of the survey instrument.
2. *Clearinghouse for Internships and International Personnel Exchange at* http://www.lawsch.uga.edu/fcil/clearintro.html (last visited Dec. 15, 1999).

APPENDIX 1

AMERICAN ASSOCIATION OF LAW LIBRARIES (AALL)
FOREIGN, COMPARATIVE AND INTERNATIONAL LAW LIBRARIES (FCIL)
SIS
CLEARINGHOUSE FOR INTERNSHIPS & INTERNATIONAL PERSONNEL EXCHANGES

1. Name and address of institution:
2. Telephone, fax, e-mail:
3. Name of contact person (please include telephone and e-mail address if any):
4. Are your willing to host an exchange or a visitor?
5. For what length of time?
6. Is your library able to negotiate support in either of the following areas?
   Salary [ ] Housing [ ]
7. What type of administrative support can you provide?
   Supervisor/mentor [ ]
   Desk place [ ]
   Assigned duties [ ]
8. Would a visitor primarily be involved with
   Public services [ ]
   Technical services [ ]
   Optional [ ]
9. What languages are spoken on your staff?
10. What is the concentration or specialization of your collection?
11. What benefit might your library draw from an exchange or visitor?
12. Has your library had any experience with exchanges or visitor? (please describe)

Please mail, fax or e-mail this survey to:

David McFadden
Southwestern University School of Law Library
Los Angeles, CA 90005-3992
USA
Tel: (213) 738-6726
Fax: (213) 738-5792
E-mail: dmcfadden@swlaw.edu

From South to North: Discoveries in the Common Law World

Pat Northey

SUMMARY. Law librarians must develop a sixth sense to catch whispers in the wind and cultivate a sense of impending developments. Changes must be perceived before they happen. The increasing globalization in the law and the legal profession was perceived by the author in 1987 in New Zealand, and she details the steps taken to enable her to deal with them. These included working for a semester in an academic library in the United States, attendance at the Canadian Law Librarians Conference, and a locum as a law librarian in a Canadian law firm. The Northern American experience was invaluable in assisting the author in using the relevant legal sources and their tools that could then be applied back in New Zealand. The generic common law bond which binds these jurisdictions meant that developments in the one legal system could then be extrapolated back and related to the New Zealand situation. The author also provides hints to assist other law librarians seeking similar enrichment.

Some might call it a reaction to a mid-library career crisis. I prefer to call it a reasoned response to the well-honed sixth sense of a professional law librarian. Call it what you will, my decision to uproot myself from the comfort of my law firm library in the southern hemisphere and to venture into a completely unknown northern hemisphere law library environment was both exciting and daunting. So why did I need to make the decision in the first place?

Pat Northey is a freelance legal researcher with 30 years' law librarian experience.

[Haworth co-indexing entry note]: "From South to North: Discoveries in the Common Law World." Northey, Pat. Co-published simultaneously in *Legal Reference Services Quarterly* (The Haworth Information Press, an imprint of The Haworth Press, Inc.) Vol. 18, No. 3, 2000, pp. 59-67; and: *Law Librarians Abroad* (ed: Janet Sinder) The Haworth Information Press, an imprint of The Haworth Press, Inc., 2000, pp. 59-67. Single or multiple copies of this article are available for a fee from The Haworth Document Delivery Service [1-800-342-9678, 9:00 a.m. - 5:00 p.m. (EST). E-mail address: getinfo@haworthpressinc.com].

By 1987, I had been working in law firms and in the university law library in a number of roles for the previous 19 years. My then present position as the library manager gave me the opportunity to do some serious strategic planning for the future, not only for the firm's library but also for my own professional development. New Zealand, just like the United States, Canada, and Australia, is a common law country, and her dependence on English law was really just starting to be eroded by the influences of the other common law jurisdictions, which had developed their "own" jurisprudence much earlier than New Zealand. In addition, England had joined the European Common Market, thereby reducing the relevance of many of her precedents for the New Zealand situation, and New Zealand was turning to "other" common law jurisdictions for persuasive decisions.

It was obvious to me that New Zealand legal practice was already, and would be increasingly, looking to the United States for case law. As a law librarian, my need to use more U.S. material meant that I first had to understand the completely different-looking footnotes and case cites, as well as Shepardizing the case law. New Zealand was not backward; we had Lexis-Nexis, but we did not have access to any training for its use. More and more Commonwealth material was being added to it which I needed to access, but Lexis-Nexis was a very expensive database to use, and I had to know how to get the information that I needed at the most reasonable cost.

Quite apart from the U.S., Canadian jurisprudence was becoming increasingly important for New Zealand. In many instances, Canadian jurisprudence acts as a conduit for U.S. law, making it immediately accessible to New Zealand lawyers. As later years would show, many of the bold directions taken by New Zealand law are directly attributable to Canadian influence.[1]

Having decided on the need to "internationalize" my law library skills, I then set about deciding where I should go and how to get there. In my mind, there was only one way to decide the "where" and that was through a systematic approach. There is nothing like a large sheet of paper and a pencil when faced with life-changing decisions! I sat down with my paper and pencil and drew a grid of all the jurisdictions that impinged on New Zealand law. It was predictably the big four–Australia, the United Kingdom, Canada, and the United States. I had a good working knowledge of finding the law in the first three jurisdictions, and I knew little about the fourth–so that appeared to answer the question of where to go.

Having belonged to the American Association of Law Librarians for many years, I was aware that it had a subcommittee on international exchanges and that Laurie Flynn was the incumbent Chair of that committee.[2] I wrote to Laurie and she went out of her way to find something for me. She tried for a placement in a number of locations, but no one wanted an exchange, so she found a Library Director who was willing to take me on. The result was that Igor Kavass of the Alyne Queener Massey Law Library at Vanderbilt offered me a student slot.

I then set about finding funding, approaching both my firm and the local publishers. The fact that I had gone about things logically and systematically definitely counted positively when I produced my begging bowl. The money angle sorted out, and the only thing left was the official paperwork. My offer from Vanderbilt supported a J2 visa application, and in no time, my dream was actually happening.

I started at Vanderbilt in January of 1987, just after the New Year. In New Zealand, everything is programmed to start from the beginning of the calendar year. But arriving in the United States in January made me understand, for the first time, how the northern hemisphere starts the new business year in September. It was already the second semester. It was winter and that was new. To be in snow and see icicles on the eaves of the dormitory I stayed in smacked of the fairy tales of childhood for me. Having come from the temperate climate of Auckland, New Zealand, I had no experience with snow.

There I was, all bright-eyed and keen to learn, but no one appeared to know what to do with me. The office I was to occupy was filled with cartons and cartons of EC official documents. I had never seen these before, but, as I could not move into the room until they were prepared for binding, I soon acquired a very close familiarity with the structure of the *Official Journal*. To tell the truth, I was so mad about having to do this (I wanted U.S. not EC experiences!) that I processed them in double quick time. This brought home to me very vividly the benefit of having a diverse library work history. I had previously worked in a university law library and was familiar with preparing large amounts of journal material for binding. That job done, I moved into my office.

After a few weeks, it appeared that no one was able to offer a suggestion about the program I should undertake, so I came up with my own. In the morning, I would attend the Administrative Law class and work my way through the first year students' legal bibliography questions, and in the afternoon I would shelf read the foreign collection. I also unpacked and shelved the government documents that came to the library, as it was a depository library. The shelf reading did make a small contribution to the bar-coding project underway in the library when I arrived. The library was bar-coding the entire collection and needed the OCLC records tied in with their actual shelf holdings.

That largely took care of my weeks; whenever I could I delved into reference works and absorbed as much as I could on the American way of law. The weekends were devoted to playing with Lexis and learning how the databases worked. No local representative was anywhere in sight. That was not so much an issue here as I could at least invest time on Lexis at Vanderbilt; when Lexis was used in New Zealand, every second cost the firm. I explored the database by starting with what I knew. My firm had just been involved with a case concerning judicial review of a commission of inquiry. It had gone to the Privy Council, and all the language of judicial review was very near to the surface of my consciousness–so my exploration initially centered around the topic of judicial review.

It was great to audit the Administrative Law class, as I had done the same in New Zealand and found many similarities in the law. A few of the topics were not yet relevant to New Zealand, but I knew they would appear there in time. The introduction of the Mixed Member Proportional representation form of government created an environment for the development of an area of practice called Public Law, where the topics learned about in that class are now happening in New Zealand, and has, in fact, accelerated their reception. Regulation/negotiation is one of these areas. It was enormously advantageous when I returned to New Zealand to have a jump-start on these new legal developments.

WHAT WAS DIFFERENT?

Language and terminology and the New Zealand accent made me stand out as foreign and gave rise to the inevitable linguistic *faux pas*. Most memorable of these was the grave mistake of asking the Library Director's male secretary for a "rubber" when, of course, I meant an eraser. *Crocodile Dundee* was showing in U.S. cinemas whilst I was at

Vanderbilt, and everyone insisted that I was really an Australian (not at all complimentary for a New Zealander!).

Of course, no "away" experience is devoid of the not-quite-so-positive side of the house. I certainly experienced a number of what I call "dis-ease" factors:

- Sudden isolation from all that is familiar. Southern and northern hemispheres are very different. The weather, accents, and way of life offer new challenges. No family to turn, or to talk, to.
- Not being able to anticipate the effect of this isolation on me.
- Going into a library with friction between heads of two services meant that there were divided staff loyalties and depleted staff energy levels. The result of this friction was that there was no real space for a foreigner.
- Not knowing where the supermarket was or how to get there.
- Not knowing that salt on the ground for snow destroyed leather boots!
- Trying to sleep in a student dormitory with a room opposite the bathroom and the telephone, and not knowing about earplugs!
- Not seeing Polynesian or Maori faces and finding out just what that meant to me.

In retrospect, I cannot really view these dis-eases as negatives. The whole experience was a learning curve, and I am now far more conscious of tangential factors that have the potential of diminishing new experiences.

WHAT DID I LEARN?

- My most illuminating experience was my introduction to *Bieber*,[3] the greatest publication to come out of the Vanderbilt Law Library. Thanks to *Bieber*, I can now proofread, and cite correctly, most U.S. footnotes in manuscripts.
- The Code and the Public Law do tie up and make sense (forgive a foreigner's ignorance).
- The *Shepard's* volumes were marvelous, an eye-opener.
- *American Jurisprudence* is a great publication.
- Lexis is a magnificent tool.
- CCH is reliably the same in every jurisdiction–a most welcome discovery.

If I had to state objectively what I found to be of the most use to me from my American experience, I would unhesitatingly list:

- The people I met, some of whom I am still in contact with twelve years later.
- Comprehending the look and feel of U.S. legal material.
- The Administrative Law lectures.

After six months, my time at Vanderbilt was up. But I was not ready to go home yet–there was still more to experience and learn. I had heard about the Canadian Law Librarians' conference which was about to take place, so I went on up to Canada. At the conference, I was offered a short-term job in a Toronto law firm. The library manager was going on maternity leave and a library minder was required. Walking back into a law firm library was like putting on an old familiar coat. Everything felt so comfortable. The firm operated in a way I knew inherently. The partners were the same kind of partners found in a New Zealand law firm; the politics of the firm were the same; and the power brokers were the same. The firm had the usual complement of articling clerks all striving and learning. Only the jurisdiction was different, but I did not feel different in this one.

It was a pleasure introducing New Zealand and Australian sources to the library. As Canada was just getting a new competition statute, it was useful to find the Competition Bureau had recruited a very helpful Australian official from the Trade Practices Commission in Australia. There are many cross-over areas between New Zealand, Australian, and Canadian law. This is why working in New Zealand is such fun. Our competition law came from Australia, Australia's came from the United States, and Canada had a similar statute. This consanguinity gives the legal researcher heaps more cases from which to choose. Canada has its Charter, and New Zealand's Bill of Rights finds its basis in the Charter. New Zealand now has the Personal Property Securities Act that is based on the Saskatchewan and New Brunswick statutes. These relate directly back to the 1962 and 1972 American Uniform Commercial Code. This allows us to pick from the Commonwealth and United States depending on the case or statute that needs supporting.

I found my New Zealand experiences invaluable whilst working in the Toronto firm; they enabled me to see analogies between their law and mine. The Canadian publishers were a little startled by my arrival and probably quite glad when I left. I am a firm believer in straight talking, like many New Zealanders, and I fear this trait may not have endeared me to all the publishers.

Canada gave me some new discoveries:

- Parliamentary bills were customarily referred to by number (like B-56).
- Federal regulations were published in the *Canada Gazette Pt II*.
- QuickLaw provided a national legal database collection.
- The *Report on Business* provided a daily news feed from the *Globe and Mail*, a national newspaper. I was not to see a similar service in New Zealand until the New Zealand Press Association started on the Knowledge Basket[4] in 1994. Now we have Newsroom and Scoop as well.
- Canadian law was also accessible via Lexis, and 12 years later more has been added.

After my six months in Toronto were up, I returned home to New Zealand, mentally and professionally enriched. A year out of one's comfort zone forces one to revisit old thinking processes and to stretch previously self-imposed limitations. My northern hemisphere year has left me with sustained ongoing benefits:

- Knowing how to approach the *U.S. Code Annotated* and the West Digest and reports.
- Knowing how to read American footnotes.
- Knowing Canadian bills are identified by letter and number.
- Being able to correspond with colleagues in both countries.
- Knowing the benefits of Lexis and QuickLaw.
- Finding earplugs.
- Walking among history.

Ten (or 11) tips for those wishing to experience law librarianship overseas:

1. Clarify in your own mind why you want to go. A clear, definitive list of objectives will help you get the most out of the experience.
2. Prioritize these objectives so you do not lose focus.
3. Choose your destination carefully and logically.

4. Enlist support, be it financial or moral, to help you get to your chosen destination. Do not be afraid to approach acquaintances or colleagues for assistance. They are far more likely to assist if you can show you have "done your homework" first (that is, numbers one to three of this list).
5. Make sure you subscribe to a law librarians' listserve in your proposed destination country before you go. This will give you insights into their current issues and, more importantly, you will have the opportunity to meet your new colleagues virtually.
6. Read up on your destination country so you can lessen the "culture shock" and find out if someone will be able to help you come to grips with local living. Not many people think to tell you about the location of the nearest supermarket or what times various shops/services close.
7. Be aware that the legal terminology is likely to be different. Make sure one of your first questions is: "Where is your citation guide?"
8. Make sure that you have had as wide an experiential range of library skills as you possibly can. You may be called on to perform tasks you do not normally undertake in your present role.
9. Maximize your opportunities whilst you are overseas. Build networks with colleagues; experience as much law librarianship as you can.
10. Be prepared to speak up for yourself. Do not always wait for your host library to suggest what tasks you can perform. Check out the possibilities and be prepared to make your own suggestions.
11. Take earplugs.

Would I do it again? Definitely. Would I change anything? Yes. I wish now that I had woken up to this opportunity earlier in my career–and perhaps more opportunities might have followed. But, in fairness to myself, this type of international law library placement had not been undertaken by any New Zealander before me, and I guess timing is everything. I went at the right time for both my firm and me. I am enriched with skills and memories. I find great professional satisfaction in passing on the knowledge I acquired to the next generation of law librarians. My final advice? Grab the brass ring with both hands . . . and don't forget the earplugs!

NOTES

1. Some of these will be alluded to later in this article.

2. *See* David L. McFadden, *The Clearinghouse for Internships and International Personnel Exchanges*, *Legal Ref. Serv. Q.*, Vol. 18, no. 3, 2000, *at* 49, for more information on this committee.

3. Mary Miles Prince, *Bieber's Dictionary of Legal Citations* (5th ed. 1997).

4. *The Knowledge Basket*, *at* http://www.knowledge-basket.co.nz (last visited Sept. 26, 2000).

An Australian Law Librarian's Experience in London

Vanessa O'Meara

SUMMARY. This article details the author's experience as the fortunate incumbent of the second Visiting Fellowship in Law Librarianship at the Institute of Advanced Legal Studies, University of London, during the summer of 1999. The experience, one of the most rewarding of the author's career, was a unique combination of teaching and learning. The most satisfying outcome of the experience was to see the birth this year of www.bailli.org, providing free access to British and Irish legal information, with the assistance of the Australian Legal Information Institute. The development of such a service was the main research interest of the author during the fellowship, and to see its inception so soon far exceeded expectations and proves that this is the type of international cooperation that the Institute fellowships can foster. An edited version of this article is being simultaneously published in 7 *Australian Law Librarian* 281 (1999). *[Article copies available for a fee from The Haworth Document Delivery Service: 1-800-342-9678. E-mail address: <getinfo@haworthpressinc.com> Website: <http://www.HaworthPress.com> © 2000 by The Haworth Press, Inc. All rights reserved.]*

As an English-born Australian, I have long been fascinated by the common law origins of the Australian legal system. When an opportunity came up to apply to spend some time working in a law library in London, I was extremely excited by the prospect.

From April until August 1999, I was lucky enough to hold the second Visiting Fellowship in Law Librarianship at the Institute of

---

Vanessa O'Meara is Reader Services Manager, Law Courts Library, Sydney, Australia.

[Haworth co-indexing entry note]: "An Australian Law Librarian's Experience in London." O'Meara, Vanessa. Co-published simultaneously in *Legal Reference Services Quarterly* (The Haworth Information Press, an imprint of The Haworth Press, Inc.) Vol. 18, No. 3, 2000, pp. 69-75; and: *Law Librarians Abroad* (ed: Janet Sinder) The Haworth Information Press, an imprint of The Haworth Press, Inc., 2000, pp. 69-75. Single or multiple copies of this article are available for a fee from The Haworth Document Delivery Service [1-800-342-9678, 9:00 a.m. - 5:00 p.m. (EST). E-mail address: getinfo@haworthpressinc.com].

Advanced Legal Studies, University of London. I first saw the Fellowship advertised in the *New Zealand Law Journal* at the end of 1997. My application required a detailed CV, letters of support from referees, an outline of my research interests, and how they related to the interests of the Institute. The Institute offers a number of fellowships to legal professionals each year, usually held by judges and academic lawyers. The Visiting Fellowship in Law Librarianship is a relatively new initiative and a very welcome opportunity for the profession of law librarianship.

The Institute of Advanced Legal Studies was founded in 1947 after half a century or more of discussion. It was originally conceived and funded as a national academic institution and that remains its prime mission today. Although constitutionally part of the University of London, its role is to support and promote legal research throughout the U.K.[1]

I was advised of my selection for the fellowship in February 1998, but felt more than a little unsure of my prospective role at the Institute. Fortunately, I was able to visit Jules Winterton, Librarian at the Institute of Advanced Legal Studies, in September 1998, prior to taking up the fellowship, while attending conferences in the U.K. We discussed arrangements for my forthcoming visit, which settled my slight apprehension. On arrival at the Institute, I was made to feel very welcome as part of the IALS library staff.

As an Australian law librarian, I felt immediately at home in the Institute Library, which is the largest law library in the U.K. Our common law heritage explains the similarity of legal materials, and I found myself amongst familiar titles of law reports, textbooks, and journals. During my time at the Institute Library, I was able to avail myself of substantial hands-on experience with both United Kingdom and European Union legal materials, plus those of a great many other jurisdictions. I was able to go straight behind the reference desk and to work!

I soon found myself at home with the collection, assisting with clients' inquiries, both by phone and in person at the inquiry counter. Many CD products were common to both my home library in Sydney and the Institute Library in London. *Current Legal Information* by Sweet & Maxwell and Wilson's *Index to Legal Periodicals*, to name just two, were well-known familiars. In addition, there was Lexis, and, of course, the World Wide Web. The Institute's catalogue was Innopac, whilst my home library uses Dynix. I found it interesting to learn to use a new system and was able to identify with the feelings of new staff and trainees starting work in my library in Sydney.

I was extremely impressed by the breadth of the Institute's international collection. I noted material from jurisdictions which are very difficult to access in Australia. The extensive research collection at the Institute covers U.K. law, European law, European Union law, United States law, Commonwealth law, and international law. For details of the commercial information services, particularly the distance access document delivery service, offered by the Institute Library, see the Institute Library's Web site.[2]

Some of the inquiries I undertook involved the use of Nigerian legislation, statutory instruments from Guernsey, legislation from Jamaica, and from the Turks and Caicos Islands, and equal opportunity laws in Northern Ireland, as well as the more familiar Australian, Canadian, and U.S. materials.

As one of my major areas of interest and research whilst in the U.K. was the provision of legal information electronically, I met with members of the Court Service (an executive agency of the Lord Chancellor's Department which provides administrative support to courts and tribunals in England and Wales), in particular senior library staff, and those responsible for the creation and maintenance of the Court Service Web site.[3] In addition, I was asked to provide feedback on the Web site, including what type of information we in Australia would like to access via the Web Site. I had similar meetings in Dublin with staff of the Courts Service there and was able to preview their Web site, which was launched in November of this year.[4]

Having spent some time behind the inquiry desk at the Supreme Court Library, at the Royal Courts of Judicature, I noticed a reassuring similarity between inquiries received there and at the Law Courts Library in Sydney. Among the patrons were litigants themselves, needing a great deal of staff assistance; ushers rushing in from court for books the judge needed urgently; and young judicial assistants fresh out of university, who were appointed to a judge for about a year, needing help with research.

There are, however, significant differences in the way primary legal materials are provided. For example, there is a very different attitude between our two countries to the provision of information free via the

Internet. The amount of United Kingdom case law, in particular, available free of charge via the Internet was very limited at that time.[5]

Australian law librarians are highly regarded in the U.K., and everywhere I went, U.K. law librarians volunteered praise of AustLII, the Australasian Legal Information Institute, which provides free access to a great deal of Australian primary legal materials through its case and statute law databases.[6] Statistics for AustLII usage in 1998 revealed 3.25 million accesses to AustLII's case law databases, or an average of 9,000 per day. It is also interesting to note that there was identifiable access to nearly 75,000 Australian cases from the United Kingdom in 1998. This raises the question: "what did U.K. lawyers and librarians do to access Australian cases before AustLII?"

During my stay in the U.K., I was invited to present a paper at the British and Irish Association of Law Librarians Conference in Glasgow in June. BIALL conferences are held annually and are extremely well attended. That year's conference attracted almost half of the total number of BIALL members, with over 400 delegates attending the weekend meeting. The conference was accompanied by the usual trade exhibition and a full evening program. Social activities included an evening of Scottish dancing, which was great fun, although I'm glad that no photographs of me dancing the Gay Gordons seem to have surfaced!

The BIALL Conference was entitled "Competencies, Changes and Challenges to the Legal Information Profession," and the organizers aimed to combine sessions addressing the current challenges facing the profession of law librarianship with those dealing with the skills and competencies needed by today's information professional.

The session I spoke at was a panel discussion about charging for legal library and information services, and I gave a sketch about the position in Australia in the twenty-five minutes available to me. The aim of the session was to examine how different law library sectors were dealing with the issue of charging for time and services. One of the threads I followed in my paper was to promote discussion and debate by contrasting the position in Australia and the U.K. regarding the provision of primary legal materials freely via the Internet, in particular via AustLII. I was also invited to be a guest speaker at the annual Court Service library staff meeting in London, which is attended by circuit court library staff from around the U.K., and which afforded me an excellent network of contacts!

In addition, I spoke at an evening seminar on Australian law in London, conducted an Australian legal resources workshop in Dublin, and a series of five workshops in London. These were attended by law librarians from such organisations as Trinity College, Dublin; University of Limerick; University of Cambridge Law Library; Lincolns Inn Library; Inner Temple Library; the Supreme Court Library, London; the Four Courts Library, Dublin; the British Library, and a variety of leading London law firms.

I must admit to envy of some of the opportunities available to U.K. law librarians. An example is their annual three day visit to the European Parliament in Brussels, an initiative of the City Law Librarians Group.

A particular achievement of my time in London was to negotiate free access to U.K. judgments. The U.K. Court Service has awarded the contract for court reporting to a London-based company called Smith Bernal. Smith Bernal in turn provides copies of the approved judgments on its Casetrack Web site at a charge of 20 pounds sterling per decision. However, I took the opportunity to visit the company, and was successful in negotiating free access for Australian Federal and Supreme Court judges and their staff to Casetrack.[7]

In November 1999, a meeting entitled "Free the Law" took place in London. It was jointly sponsored by a number of organizations, including the Institute of Advanced Legal Studies, the Society for Computers and the Law, and the British and Irish Association of Law Librarians. Professor Graham Greenleaf of AustLII had asked for my assistance in setting up an opportunity for him to give a paper in London. Through various contacts I had made in London, and much lobbying of people in positions of influence to effect the development of free Web-based legal information, I was able to assist him. According to Jules Winterton, the meeting was attended by a "high powered audience from government, practitioners and judiciary of around 200 with unanimous agreement. Very complimentary about AustLII. There is quite a groundswell to do something similar which we are trying to build on between IALS and University of Warwick."[8]

The interim name for the concept was UKELELI! It has now been renamed BAILII, which stands for British and Irish Legal Information Institute, providing free access to British and Irish legal information. The site is now live at http://www.bailii.org, using software and technical support provided by AustLII. BAILII is growing fast and is living proof that the "Access to Justice" reforms in the U.K now support maximizing access to the law's raw materials of that country, without charge, via the World Wide Web.

The Visiting Fellowship unfortunately does not include any salary component, so it is a matter of persuading your employer to fund you or of funding yourself. However, at the Institute, I had all the facilities available to a senior member of staff: computer, Internet access, e-mail account, photocopying, telephone, and fax.

The experience was one of the most rewarding of my career and is well worth pursuing if your circumstances permit. After more than twenty years in the profession here in Sydney, it was a wonderful experience to be extended and challenged by the opportunity to work in another country. There was also tremendous satisfaction in being able to contribute to the work of another organization in a different jurisdiction. The unique combination of teaching and learning was exciting indeed.

Practical details, such as housing, were made easier by access to the University of London's accommodation Web site. I was able to negotiate a very satisfactory rental of a small flat right in central London, ten minutes walk from the University, which was owned by an academic at the University who was off to Athens on sabbatical for almost the exact and corresponding period I was to spend in London. Jules Winterton, the Institute's Librarian, very kindly provided me with the necessary reference to the apartment's owner. Everything was provided, including a computer with Internet access. My two teenage children visited me in their mid-year school holidays and were thrilled to find Internet access at my home. My 16-year-old daughter immediately began "chatting" to her friends at home in Sydney!

Thanks are due to Jules Winterton and his staff at the Institute, who made me so very welcome, and to Sally Phillips, Librarian at the Supreme Court, Royal Courts of Justice, and Stuart Cole, Head of Library and Information Support Services of the Court Service, who were most accommodating of my requests to experience an insider's view of their working environment. Joe Donnelly of the Four Courts Library and Jennefer Aston of the Bar Council, Dublin, were both extremely hospitable and facilitated an excellent and informative program for me. Finally, my manager Lesley O'Loughlin and my colleagues here at the Law Courts Library also deserve a vote of thanks for cheerfully putting up with my five-month absence!

I recommend the Visiting Fellowship in Law Librarianship at the Institute of Advanced Legal Studies as an exciting, challenging, and very worthwhile opportunity.

NOTES

1. Extensive information about the Institute, and its fellowship program, can be found on its Web site *at* http://www.sas.ac.U.K./ials (last visited Apr. 5, 2000).
2. *Id.*
3. *Court Service,* at http://www.courtservice.gov.uk/ (last visited Sept. 25, 2000).
4. *Courts Service*, at http://www.courts.ie at (last visited Sept. 25, 2000).
5. *See* discussion of the new BAILII Web site, *infra*.
6. *See Australian Legal Information Institute at* http://www.austlii.edu.au (last visited Apr. 5, 2000).
7. To access Casetrack, clients must first register for a password. Charges are made only per decision downloaded. For further information, *see* http://www.smithbernal.com. Decisions available are Court of Appeal and Crown Office judgments from April 96-present and High Court judgments from July 98-present. Prior to this date, Court of Appeal decisions are available on Lexis. For judgments not available on Lexis, the best option is to get in touch with the appropriate Circuit librarian, who could suggest the best way of accessing the decision, or perhaps assist in obtaining it. The official advice is to apply to the appropriate court reporting service to purchase a copy of the required decision.
8. The transcript of the meeting is available *Society for Computers & Law, at* http://www.scl.org (last visited Apr. 5, 2000).

Abroad Thoughts from Home*

Mary-Rose Russell

SUMMARY. Law librarianship is international although international law library experience is normally gained away from one's own legal system. The author, who has law degrees from both New Zealand and Zimbabwe, changed to law librarianship whilst living in South Africa. Her legal training in two very different legal systems enabled her to use the tools of law in both systems. Having become very comfortable in the African environment, the author returned to her country of origin, which now felt like a foreign jurisdiction. She details the journey of leaving the known, leaving security, and finding people she knew would help. She shows why moving outside the square is mandatory for your professional life. *[Article copies available for a fee from The Haworth Document Delivery Service: 1-800-342-9678. E-mail address: <getinfo@haworthpressinc.com> Website: <http://www.HaworthPress.com> © 2000 by The Haworth Press, Inc. All rights reserved.]*

"It's the exception that proves the rule . . ." is a well-worn English adage. Librarians wanting to have international experience normally set about organizing this from the security of their own country. Obviously, I had not taken the rule to heart when I decided to embark on a career in law librarianship. . . .

I suppose that my career has been a little unusual in that I traded in my life as a practising barrister and solicitor in New Zealand, where I was enmeshed in the English common law, and turned to law librarianship whilst pursuing a love affair with Southern Africa. The upshot

---

Mary-Rose Russell is Library Manager, Davis Law Library University, Auckland, New Zealand.

*With apologies to Robert Browning.

[Haworth co-indexing entry note]: "Abroad Thoughts from Home." Russell, Mary-Rose. Co-published simultaneously in *Legal Reference Services Quarterly* (The Haworth Information Press, an imprint of The Haworth Press, Inc.) Vol. 18, No. 3, 2000, pp. 77-83; and: *Law Librarians Abroad* (ed: Janet Sinder) The Haworth Information Press, an imprint of The Haworth Press, Inc., 2000, pp. 77-83. Single or multiple copies of this article are available for a fee from The Haworth Document Delivery Service [1-800-342-9678, 9:00 a.m. - 5:00 p.m. (EST). E-mail address: getinfo@haworthpressinc.com].

was that I completed my degree in Library and Information Science via correspondence from the University of South Africa. The next step was working as a law librarian in a completely different legal system–this time a Roman-Dutch based one. This was not as suicidal as it sounds, as I had also been admitted as an Advocate at the Zimbabwean Bar and had *per force* to come to grips with the basics of a Roman-Dutch legal system.

Still, passing requalification examinations, even via a post-graduate degree, does not guarantee a solid working knowledge of the resources available to a legal researcher or law librarian. I embarked on a process of easing myself into Roman-Dutch law librarianship by taking on short-term contract work in a variety of libraries with legal collections, so that I could acquaint myself with the myriad of available resources. My biggest life-line was the Organization of South African Law Libraries (OSALL). Joining it was definitely the smartest move I made. There I met up with truly professional law librarians who were unstintingly generous with their time and advice. I have vivid memories of sitting at my desk in a law firm library battling with an obscure old manual, telephone in one hand, and being talked through the use of the manual by one of my senior colleagues. Nothing can repay the gratitude I feel for such help.

So I became habituated to law librarianship in a foreign jurisdiction, which by that time did not really feel foreign at all. I worked my way through law firms' libraries and finally settled at Service Unit Law, the law library at the University of Pretoria. This was a challenge in itself in that I had to acquire another language, and whilst I never got to anything like the fluent stage, by the time I left, I could understand, read, and converse in Afrikaans. At the University, I expanded my repertoire to include international and comparative law librarianship, and everything seemed settled and stable, until–20 years after leaving New Zealand–I heard the siren call of "home," and that only happened because I was following one of my long-held tenets.

I am an ardent advocate of law librarians establishing links and networks with colleagues not only nationally but also internationally. These international networks are essential tools for a successful law librarian. To this end, I subscribe to a number of law librarian listserves and actively establish contacts in other parts of the world. It was through the medium of the listserv that I became aware of the Asia Pacific Health, Special and Law Librarians Conference scheduled to be held in Perth in 1997. I submitted a couple of papers, which were accepted, organized my funding, and off I went to Perth, which ultimately provided my "open sesame."

At the Perth Conference, I made many new contacts and friends. My New Zealand contacts I strengthened on a post-conference trip home. My first impressions of New Zealand law librarianship were most favorable, and, as a result, I was very receptive to the idea of returning to New Zealand to work.

So, what I regard as *my* international experience is my present role as the Library Manager at the Davis Law Library at the University of Auckland, New Zealand. Here, I have come full circle these 20 years later. Leaving the security of the South African Roman-Dutch legal system, with its treasures of multi-lingual Old Authorities, a strong base of customary law, and its exhilarating developments in constitutional and human rights law, to return to an English common law jurisdiction was not an easy decision.

Now, using the law of my own legal system by birth and training, I feel a little like *E.T.* at times. Taking on the mantle of Library Manager means I do not have the luxury safety net of being able to tiptoe into my international experience. Ignorance is no excuse; I am expected to know, and rightly so. My returning to an academic law library has made the transition easier. It is getting to grips again with the nitty gritty of black letter law that provides the real challenge. My training for the legal profession in New Zealand did not include many legal research skills, and not being trained in law librarianship in my own country, I am constantly challenged, and ever wary of my automatic response because I have consciously to think twice about which jurisdiction I am now in.

Once again, I have turned to my colleagues, this time in the New Zealand Law Librarians' Group, and, once again, I have been overwhelmed by the generosity and support I have received. In addition, I set about reading the basic texts on the New Zealand law. In the 20 years that I have been away, there have been an astonishing number of changes in New Zealand jurisprudence; the courts changed their names, and there have been major developments in the commercial sphere, as well as in constitutional and administrative law.

I have found it helpful to conduct training sessions for new staff. It is one way of ensuring that I know my way around various sources.

Each and every day brings new learning dimensions, and it is very much a roller-coaster ride–a controlled one, though.

I realize that my experience is quite different from other law librarians who do not wish to make their international experience a long-term affair. However, I have a long list of dos and don'ts that have worked either for me or for colleagues–others may find these useful when considering any form of international law librarian experience.

DOs

- Before you start thinking of international experience, make sure you are an active participant in your law librarians' group. Share your knowledge willingly, and others will reciprocate. Join relevant listserves, your own national one and some selected international ones. This way you can imbibe the legal flavor of other countries.
- Read the different international law librarian journals or publications. These are excellent sources of information.
- Keep your eye on law librarian conferences and make plans to attend an international one. These provide unsurpassed opportunities for meeting colleagues and building networks.
- Find out if there are any formal exchange programs for law librarians and if so, contact them for assistance.
- Always take the opportunity to learn new skills. You never know when you may need them. Law librarians generally need to be jills-of-all-trades.
- Decide where you want to go and why. Also decide which sort of experience you are looking for–is it law firm, academic, or corporate? Establish contact with law librarians in that country and find out who will be the best person to help you out.
- Do your homework. Will your present employer allow you to undertake extended experiential work overseas or will you need to resign? Will you need to get a visa? What are living expenses like in the country you propose to visit? How difficult will it be to get reasonable accommodation? What will the weather be like?
- Write up a funding proposal. Market your plan and seek financial assistance from your employer, local legal publishing houses, your law librarian group, and other funding agencies. The more you show that you are driving the process and are serious about

it, the more you will be supported. Offer to provide feedback, written or oral, to all your sponsors.

- Try to combine your time overseas with a law librarian conference. This will maximize your experience.
- Once overseas, be generous with your knowledge, and offer to teach your host organization about law librarianship in your country.
- Be prepared to undertake any reasonable task that is requested of you.
- Take every single opportunity to extend your knowledge base. Read the local student texts, attend any lectures that may be on offer.
- Be prepared for some form of culture shock. It is a natural response to being in strange or different surroundings. Allow yourself time to adjust.
- Keep notes of your experiences as you go along. If you have to produce a report when you return home, it is so much easier if you have written notes to work from. It is almost impossible to remember all the interesting things that happen during an extended away stay.
- Enjoy the experience to the fullest.
- Maintain contact with your foreign colleagues.
- Write a "thank-you" letter afterwards. This way you could smooth the path for other "foreign" colleagues who may want to work at the same place.

DON'Ts

- Don't banish thoughts of international experience because "that happens for other people but not for me." It is a great experience for everyone.
- Don't expect others to make your dream come true. You have to do all the hard work yourself. That is not to say you cannot call on others for help and advice, but in the long run it is up to you to achieve your goal.
- Don't be too shy or ashamed to ask for help or information. After all, the whole exercise is about learning new skills, and the experience begins the moment you have made up your mind to go.

- Don't forget to get as much information about the place you are going to as you can absorb. What season will it be? What is the current exchange rate with your local currency? Will you need to acquire any new skills before you go–like skating? What about medical insurance? Do you need to take precautions against tropical diseases?
- Don't rush off overseas without first having decided on your objectives and priorities. It is remarkably easy to have a great experience and to arrive home and discover that you have not actually mastered the one specific skill for which you went overseas.
- Don't dictate to your host organization about what work you are or are not prepared to do.
- Don't criticize or constantly compare your "home" library with that of your host organization. Although it is a natural reaction to a change of circumstance, comparisons are odious, so keep away from that territory unless specifically asked.
- Don't allow your whole experience to be marred by minor irritations that inevitably occur when you are away from home.

WHAT ARE THE BENEFITS I HAVE OBTAINED FROM MY MULTI-JURISDICTIONAL EXPERIENCES?

- Perhaps the main advantage for me is that I greatly increased my marketability within our profession, and I opened up new employment opportunities for myself.
- I acquired another language and the great benefits of being able to read legal texts written in other languages.
- The Roman-Dutch based legal systems in Zimbabwe and South Africa are no longer closed books to me.
- I am able to provide a more informed reference service to some of my New Zealand clients. Many South Africans have settled in New Zealand, and I am able to assist faculty members and solicitors requiring South African law materials.
- My experience as a foreigner in a foreign legal system has given me more empathy with my foreign students.
- Intellectually I am enriched by being able to see the parallels and similarities between the Roman-Dutch and common law legal systems.
- I was made aware of the enormous benefits of taking a more comparative view of legal research.

- My horizons have expanded. I have been privileged to be part of a world that has enlarged my perspectives, both professionally and personally.
- I have made wonderful friends and established a fantastic network of colleagues.
- I have had the advantage of being in a legal publishing environment where Folio 4.2 was adopted earlier, and had seen some of its possibilities, long before its adoption into New Zealand. Experiencing what some publishers can provide makes me question other publishers who deny the possibilities.
- I have had the opportunity to meet, and listen to, some of the "big names" in the South African legal world.

Legal research, by its nature, can no longer be insular. With the increasing internationalization of law as a result of regional harmonisation or international convention or treaty, the law librarian has little choice but to internationalize her/his skills. Some skills can be learnt out of books, but nothing can take the place of experiential learning. There is a wonderful world of new opportunities and skills awaiting law librarians out there. Whether you venture into a foreign legal system or opt for a country with a similar legal system to yours, the experience is exactly what you make of it.

I can only encourage you to take a step into the unknown. You will benefit both professionally and personally. If I could offer only one small piece of advice, it would be this–never be too scared to take life's byways, you could end up on the highway to adventure.

How I Spent My Sabbatical Leave at a Korean Law Library

Heija B. Ryoo

SUMMARY. The author describes the experience of spending a sabbatical leave at the Seoul National University College of Law Library in Korea. She describes practical experiences on planning for a leave, developing project ideas, adapting to changes in a different environment, performing daily routines, and other suggestions for those who are thinking about spending a leave at a foreign law library. *[Article copies available for a fee from The Haworth Document Delivery Service: 1-800-342-9678. E-mail address: <getinfo@haworthpressinc.com> Website: <http://www.HaworthPress.com> © 2000 by The Haworth Press, Inc. All rights reserved.]*

INTRODUCTION

As a native Korean who has lived in the United States for over a quarter of a century, I was truly excited about the thought of spending a semester at a university in Korea. Visiting one's home country always brings mixed emotions of excitement, and nostalgia; you can imagine how I felt when the opportunity to work there for a semester became a reality. I spent the 1995 fall semester on a sabbatical leave at the Seoul National University (SNU) College of Law. Even though I had made numerous short trips to Korea, this was my first opportunity to stay this long since I first left Korea some 26 years ago.

Heija B. Ryoo is Director of Library Systems and Associate Professor of Law, Southern Illinois University Law Library.

[Haworth co-indexing entry note]: "How I Spent My Sabbatical Leave at a Korean Law Library." Ryoo, Heija B. Co-published simultaneously in *Legal Reference Services Quarterly* (The Haworth Information Press, an imprint of The Haworth Press, Inc.) Vol. 18, No. 3, 2000, pp. 85-99; and: *Law Librarians Abroad* (ed: Janet Sinder) The Haworth Information Press, an imprint of The Haworth Press, Inc., 2000, pp. 85-99. Single or multiple copies of this article are available for a fee from The Haworth Document Delivery Service [1-800-342-9678, 9:00 a.m. - 5:00 p.m. (EST). E-mail address: getinfo@haworthpressinc.com].

The planning for the leave grew out of a casual talk back in early 1994 with the then-Director of the Law Library at SNU, when he visited our library during a visit to Carbondale. We talked about library automation and the law library in general, and I indicated my interest in visiting his library. We continued to communicate after his return to Korea. It was at the beginning of the 1994 fall semester, close to the deadline for submitting an application for sabbatical leave for the 1995-96 academic year at Southern Illinois University (SIU), when I received an invitation from the SNU College of Law. I hurriedly applied for the sabbatical leave from SIU; the leave was subsequently approved by SIU in the spring of 1995, and I started to prepare for my leave.

The Law Library Director at SNU in Korea and I exchanged project ideas, and a projects list was informally agreed upon by late spring of 1995. (The director became the Dean of Planning and Coordination at the University in late spring.) The papers then were transferred to the College of Law Dean and the new Law Library Director. I began to gather materials relating to law library collection development, law library administration, and automated systems. I arranged for free subscription authorization for FirstSearch from OCLC, and for approval from West to access Westlaw from Korea, etc. Everything seemed to be going very smoothly until I had to deal with the Korean immigration officials for my visa. People often comment on the amount of paperwork necessary to come to the United States, but I didn't realize how stringent the paper requirements were, and how cumbersome and bureaucratic the whole process was to get a long-term-stay visa from the Korean government. It took practically the whole summer to get all the necessary papers and to get the visa (I was worried that I might not be able to make the scheduled departure date).

It was late August when I arrived in Korea. Fall had been my favorite season when I was growing up in Korea and it still was; the sky was high and deep blue, fall colors were spectacular on mountains (you can see mountains from almost every direction even in a big city like Seoul with a population of about 15 million), the water in the creeks and rivers was blue, and rice fields were filled with ripe golden colors. Another favorite of the fall season is the much celebrated "Chusuk," similar to Thanksgiving here. It is time for good food, a big get-together with relatives, and, more importantly, visits to ancestors' graves to pay respect with a formal ceremony. Of course, I was not there just for pleasure, but having a week off before I started my work at the school was memorable.

I didn't quite know what to expect in terms of office environment, the people at the college, the library condition, or the automation status of the college. Moreover, I was a little apprehensive about how I would be accepted among the faculty and staff. I had left the country so long ago, and everything has changed so much during that time. Once I got there and started working, however, I quickly became comfortable, and easily developed daily work routines.

I consider my experience unique and rewarding, and this experience might provide tips to those who are thinking about an adventurous leave at a foreign institution.

THE FIRST DAY

Immediately upon my arrival at the Law Library on the morning of my first day at the school, I met with the Law School Dean, and was informed, to my surprise, that I was supposed to be at the Law School Faculty meeting that afternoon to be introduced. I had been staying at my sister's apartment until that day, and had planned to move into the apartment on campus provided by the law school after meeting with the Dean. Because I was not dressed properly for a formal introduction, I had to return to my sister's apartment to change in time for the meeting, an almost impossible task due to the traffic jams in the streets of Seoul. We braved the Seoul traffic and barely got back in time for the meeting. (Normal 50 minute drives often stretch to 2-3 hours, cars just don't move, and it does not matter whether it is rush hour or not; in Carbondale where I live, rush hour traffic means perhaps 10 cars waiting at a traffic light.)

If your law school faculty meeting rooms are similar to SIU's, where we use one of the classrooms, you would be impressed with and envious of the SNU faculty's facility. It is a huge room with beautiful furniture arranged like a fancy corporate boardroom. The college's administrative staff members were busily preparing for the meeting, putting agenda papers on each table, and waiting outside the room while the meeting was in progress. One rather shocking thing was that there was not a single female faculty member in the entire room. I may be the first female faculty member who ever attended a faculty meeting there. Before the meeting started, the Dean introduced me with nice remarks, and I made a quick exit. Somehow the whole mood was a little too much and too overwhelming for me.

I felt totally ill prepared, but managed to get through that first day, including my move to an apartment. That was the beginning of a unique and exciting four-month experience.

THE SEOUL NATIONAL UNIVERSITY COLLEGE OF LAW

The Seoul National University is the most prestigious university in Korea, and, as in most Asian countries, legal education is an undergraduate program. The campus is nestled in the beautiful Kwanak Mountain with hills, woods, and creeks. SNU has about 1,300 undergraduate law students (the government sets entrance quotas for incoming students), and about 300 graduate-level students in law. The school's program is divided into a Department of Private Law and a Department of Public Law. The College of Law offers two advanced degrees: Master of Laws (LL.M.) and Doctor of Juridical Science (J.S.D.). There are about 32 faculty members, consisting of the nation's top legal scholars, and many of them serve as advisors on national policy matters. Almost all are graduates of Seoul National University College of Law and hold advanced degrees from Korea, Germany, or the United States. The school's alumni comprise more than 50% of the Korean Bar members, and I understand that practically all the judges and public prosecutors are SNU graduates.

The Korean legal system is based on civil law tradition. There is no degree requirement to take the national Judicial Examination to become a lawyer, so law school course work is often neglected by law students. In fact, the majority of law students spend most of their time preparing intensively for the Judicial Examination while they are in school. The competition to pass the exam is fierce and only a small portion of all graduates, about 300 out of about 6,000 annual law graduates, pass the bar examination (there is an annual quota of about 300 for passing bar exams set by the government).[1] Those who pass the bar exam go through two years of professional training at the Supreme Court's Judicial Research and Training Institute, and, upon completion of this unified training, then become judges, prosecutors, or practicing attorneys. A large number of graduates who didn't pass the bar exam end up spending many years after graduation trying again to pass the bar, but many end up in nonlegal careers. There were only 2,820 lawyers in 1994 in Korea. The often cited reasons for a stringent bar examination and for the small passage rate are to maintain professional standards and to prevent overheated competition in the profession.

After years of discussion and debate about reforming legal education, and the legal system, the government, in 1995, formally proposed an overall change to legal education and the legal profession, but it faced a strong opposition from the practicing legal community, especially the Supreme Court justices, and no significant changes have yet occurred.

SNU LAW LIBRARY

SNU College of Law is the only law school in Korea that has a separate law library building, and it has no direct connections to the other law buildings. It is a branch of the central university library system and is administered by the main library. Acquisitions, cataloging, and serials processing are all done by the main library. The law library has three support staff members, mainly for circulation and for maintaining the reference room. The Law Library Director is appointed by the Law School Dean from among the law teaching faculty for a two-year term. There are a very limited number of professional librarians even at the main university library, and there is no professional librarian assigned to the law library.

The library has open stacks; materials are classified under the Dewey decimal system; and OPAC terminals (including a network connection to the Campus Wide Information System) are available for patrons. The collection size is about 80,000 volumes of treatises, 2,000 academic journals, numerous papers, and text books on legal science and related areas. Rather than focusing on library services to patrons, the library is still very much used only as a study room by students. Individual teaching faculty office collections are often more complete and better maintained than the library collections, so most of the faculty don't use the library for their teaching or research. With the planned electronic resources library in a new building now under construction, the library's role might change in terms of providing access to electronic information, but the lack of professionally trained librarians is still a major concern.

AMERICAN LAW COLLECTION AT THE LIBRARY

Being one of the branch libraries on the campus, with a very small book budget (they would not give me the exact figures), I was told that the budget is not really a fixed amount and depends on who makes requests for purchase to the main library. The former Law Library Director is the resident expert on American law at the college, and during his tenure as director, he strengthened the American legal collection, but it was still at a very minimal level. One should not compare their collection with any American law school library collection, but if plans to change the legal training to a professional level school occur, the library collection is one area that will require major attention, even though it is often ignored and neglected in any reform plan documents.

It was nice to see such materials as *U.S. Code* sets with current pocket parts, hundreds of reporter volumes, major legal periodicals, many Restatements, and current treatises on the shelves, but even with a lack of adequate overall shelf space, the library had many superseded, outdated materials (mostly donations from faculty members) on the shelves. The government property control regulations are such that once added to the inventory, it is almost impossible to discard, or take out from the inventory list without justification.

The Dewey decimal classification scheme was used, but the major problem was that materials were under two different edition schemes. Earlier items were classified under an older Dewey edition, and newer ones with the new edition. Instead of separating materials classified under the new edition, those new ones were inter-shelved with the materials in an older edition scheme. Major reclassifications and re-shelvings are planned when the new building is completed.

One startling practice was that there were no standing orders for major legal serials except for legal journals. No wonder there were so many outdated and incomplete sets in the collection! I, of course, mentioned that American law libraries spend about 75-85% of the annual serials budget on standing orders. Delayed shipments, lost issues, lack of acquisitions expertise for standing orders, and language barriers are other causes of problems in acquisitions.

Lack of professional librarians to administer, manage, and maintain the law library seems to be the most urgent problem in my opinion, but this also seems to be the most difficult problem to remedy due to the nation's civil service system, unions, budget, and the university's personnel policy.

WORKING RELATIONSHIP WITH LAW SCHOOL DEAN

Even though I proposed a number of possible projects before I went there, I knew after several meetings with the Law School Dean that my time would be spent mainly on the law school automation project. The college had already prepared its comprehensive automation plan, and there was a committee for the project "Computerization of Legal Studies and Education." The Law School Dean is an expert in international law, especially human rights, and is very active in the United Nations' work, and is quite aware of the uses of the technology in American law schools. During his term as Dean (Deanship is a two-year term, elected by teaching faculty members), he wanted to make technological advances for the college one of his big achievements. He believed that the faculty needed to be trained in using technology to be able to teach students properly and to maintain respect from students. The Dean was very accessible, and I really enjoyed numerous discussions with him on many different topics. He was always willing to listen to my ideas and appreciated every change that I was able to make. His attitude was that the school wanted to "take out everything you know" during my stay. He supplied me with a high-end computer system, a superb assistant, and a committee of four teaching faculty members, and, above all, genuine interest and support for my work. During my stay, I worked closely with the committee members, especially with the Computer Lab Assistant. Because the Dean was a strong advocate for use of electronic resources and use of technology in teaching, it was a joy to work on the various automation projects.

THE RIGHT PLACE AT THE RIGHT TIME

The Internet was just starting to catch fire in Korea, with commercial vendors providing Internet services in early 1995. With my years of experience using electronic mail and other Internet functions and resources in my current job, I was well-suited to introduce the law school to the Internet age. Electronic mail had been used by a very small group of students and faculty on the campus before my arrival. The law school already had a computer lab for students, and some faculty members had computers in their offices, mainly for word processing. The law school had no Local Area Network, but they had just finished the direct network connection for a small number of workstations, including the one in my office,[2] right before my arrival (I heard the direct Internet connection was timed to coincide with my arrival). SNU had a Campus Wide Information System (CWIS) already in place, and access was available throughout the campus.

The law school was at a stage where they needed someone to introduce and train the law faculty to use the Internet. The Internet was fairly new to law faculty, but there was strong interest, especially from the Dean. The speed of change was incredible; the Internet heat was spreading fast over the campus and over all of Korean society. I guess in a small country the fad spreads at a faster rate, and you can feel the heat more closely. The government-run communications companies were changing to network cables, the newspapers carried Internet training advertisements from various institutions, and there were constant news items on radio and TV. The Internet developments that had taken a number of years in the States happened in a very short time in Korea: the whole society made visible efforts to catch up.

PROJECTS, PROJECTS, AND PROJECTS

Electronic Mail

The first thing I started was an e-mail connection to the staff at the SIU Law Library. The Seoul National University campus was providing electronic mail through the Campus Wide Information System, but almost no law faculty and no library staff were using e-mail. Since I had been using Eudora for e-mail at SIU, I decided to introduce this program instead of the more cumbersome e-mail program used under the CWIS system. Eudora was installed on my and the Computer Lab Assistant's computers. I applied for an e-mail account and within a couple days, it was ready. It was a relief to be able to communicate with the SIU staff through e-mail. I was in such a far away place (one gets 6,000 frequent flyer miles for one way to Korea), yet communication took place within a few seconds. I don't know how I would have worked and accomplished what I did if I hadn't had that connection to receive assistance from the staff at the SIU Law Library.

The Internet

We installed Netscape for Web browsing, the Ewan telnet program, and WS-FTP for file transfer on my computer. Internet browsing through Netscape was at a satisfactory speed, and the Telnet and the FTP programs that I used in the U.S. were also working well, so that I was fully equipped to do all the Internet functions from the first week.

Access to Online Databases

Connecting to online legal databases such as Lexis and Westlaw via dial-up was out of the question, due to telecommunications charges, so the best option was through the Internet. Before I left the U.S., I was generously given permission by West to access Westlaw from Korea for my research under the SIU Law School contract. I installed the Westlaw client software on my computer and used the database via the Internet telnet mode. I had several occasions to access legal periodicals, court cases, and regulations with satisfactory results.

Lexis service is available through a commercial company, DACOM, in Korea, but no academic subscription option is available to law schools.

I suggested that the college negotiate directly with both Westlaw and Lexis regarding academic subscription contracts, perhaps starting with very limited access to databases and with a set time period during the low usage times. (There is a 15 hour time difference, so the typical peak time in the U.S. would be the middle of the night in Korea.)

Access to the bibliographic database "WorldCat" through First-Search was also introduced to faculty and graduate students. I received a block of free search authorizations from OCLC before I left the States and additional ones in Korea from the Korean commercial company, Orom, which handled OCLC services for Korean libraries. The faculty was interested in searching for new works by particular authors in their fields, and comprehensive lists of works in specific subject fields.

Electronic Journal Subscription

Some faculty members expressed interest in a current awareness service in their fields, so I looked into the subscription option via the Internet for the *Current Index to Legal Periodicals*. The SIU Law Library had been subscribing CILP in an electronic format via the Internet for the last three years at a lower subscription price and a faster delivery of the issues than a paper subscription. I thought the Internet subscription would be an ideal solution, especially because of slow mail delivery between the two countries.

The University of Washington Law Library gave me access authorization to test the downloading of issues. The files required minor format editing, but the whole process from file transfer to printing was successful. The college placed a subscription, and I trained the law library staff to download, edit, and print the issues. I also trained the staff to send the electronic texts to those faculty members wishing to receive them in electronic format via e-mail.

Electronic Library Resources Outline

The SNU automation plan included detailed hardware configurations for the College of Law Local Area Network with connections to the SNU network and CD-ROM network, and two separate file servers. I worked on an outline for electronic resources focusing on library catalogs, online database searching, Korean legal materials, CD-ROM databases, Computer Assisted Legal Instruction materials, the Internet, the SNU home page, and networked programs and files.

This was revised several times after consulting with the Dean and committee members, and the final outline was included in my final report to the Law School Dean.

SNU Home Page

When I first proposed the idea of building the Web home page, it was too new to be accepted by the college as a priority group project. As I explained the benefits of having the home page, however, tying it to both world-wide publicity for the school and easy access to legal resources on the Internet in an organized way for faculty and students, it quickly generated interest.

Much of my time was actually spent searching and reviewing hundreds of Internet sites and organizing the information in subject groups so that the students and faculty would have an easier time accessing needed information. The home pages of Washburn, Cornell, Emory, St. Louis, and the United States House of Representatives are the ones that helped me a great deal in building sites for the college. Since most SNU users have little experience searching the Internet, I wanted to organize the information as clearly and simply as possible.

Before I went to Korea, I did some Internet searching and did presentations on searching the Internet to SIU Law Library staff, but like most of you, I couldn't afford to spend hours and hours of office time doing Internet searching. With this opportunity in Korea, I was able to go to many interesting sites and some days spent more than half of the time on Internet searching.

The Computer Lab Assistant, in the meantime, worked on getting information on Seoul National University College of Law and some Korean legal sites. We purchased books on HTML (most of the Dummies series manuals have been translated into Korean) and started converting the documents into HTML format. We started building the English version of the home page first, and gave a preview of it to the faculty when I gave a special lecture on the Legal Resources on the Internet. A more complete version was shown to the Automation Committee members right before I left, and the home page has been up on the Internet since February 1996. Since my departure, the Computer Lab Assistant has been maintaining the site nicely, adding European sites, some course materials, and a Korean version of the home page.[3]

Special Lectures

In November, I presented a special lecture on "American Law School Libraries in the Information Age and the Legal Information Resources on the Internet" to faculty and graduate students. I first briefly introduced what the law libraries do and how they manage library services in the information age, and then introduced the Internet functions and the legal sites.

By this time, almost the entire faculty had Pentium workstations in their offices, each with four basic Internet software programs. The interest from the faculty was strong, and it showed in their attendance at my lecture. I was later told that this may have been the largest faculty attendance for any type of lecture or seminar in the college in recent years.

I prepared a handout for "Legal Information Resources on the Internet," including sites on Korean legal information resources; East Asian countries' information; and information on American law schools, bar associations and organizations, law school home pages, electronic newsletters, and law journals. This was later used as the basis for the legal information resources section of the SNU College of Law home page.

The staff at the main library was also interested in the Internet, and I presented two special lectures on "Libraries in the Information Age" and "Internet Basics and Library-Related Resources on the Internet." The staff was very excited about learning to use the Internet as well as learning PowerPoint for their training presentations.

Small Group Training for the Law Faculty

The response to the Internet training sessions was overwhelming, and we scheduled four two-hour sessions using three workstations in the computer lab. Each session had about 4-6 faculty members and included hands-on training for electronic mail, Internet searching using Netscape, and online searching of FirstSearch via the telnet program. Detailed handouts were also prepared and distributed with this training.

Research

I have been working on a list of recommended Korean legal materials for a while, and this was a good opportunity for me to work on that project more extensively. One thing I discovered, however, was that the law library did not have an extensive collection of Korean law publications in English. I gathered selective lists in different subject fields, which would be incorporated into my list, and my work concentrated on Korean language materials. It was hard to comprehend how small the total number of law books published in Korea is compared with the volume of legal materials published in the United States.

One useful tool was the *Index to Korean Legal Materials* (in Korean), which was prepared by the Law Library of the College of Law at Seoul National University. This set indexes all law-related publications including monographs, theses and dissertations, journals, and serials.

Other Projects

The college is undertaking two major projects involving Korean legal materials that are worth discussing even though I didn't actually spend much time on them.

One project is the indexing of Korean legal materials under the supervision of the library staff. Three volumes were already published, and the indexing project for a fourth volume, covering 1992-1995, just began while I was there. It sounded almost an impossible project for the library to undertake, but the three previous volumes were done, and they are repeating the project for the fourth volume with three law graduate students hired from other universities.[4] The Dean was looking for a commercial company to collaborate with, but was not successful. Perhaps the company didn't see it as an economically beneficial project.

The second project is participation in the Global Legal Information Network (GLIN) sponsored by the Library of Congress. While I was there, the GLIN Project Team from the LC visited the college. This project is to build primary source materials, in both original and English languages, from all foreign countries and to make them available through the Internet. The project team was making arrangements with the Korean Assembly Library for legislative materials, the Supreme Court Library for court cases, and the SNU College for the Korean legal materials indexing project. LC is providing assistance to foreign countries, such as extensive training in areas like indexing and hardware requirements for representatives from each country, and it will be a milestone for the global legal community when this project is finished.

LAST DAY: "DO I REALLY DESERVE THIS RECOGNITION?"

My last day at the college was just two days before I left Korea. I was told that there was a faculty meeting at 12:00, and I was to attend. The meeting started with a fancy, catered lunch in the same faculty meeting room with which I was so impressed on my first day. After lunch, the Dean opened the meeting with a speech recognizing my contributions to the college. He made it sound so impressive and important that I thought, "Did I really do that much?" One of the things he mentioned was that my work was a milestone for the college's automation process, especially in introducing electronic mail and the Internet to the faculty. The whole mood was very touching, sentimental, and thoughtful.

Of course, I then continued to work, checking the last e-mail messages, deleting and copying personal files, and then went around the law library and the main library. There were many good-byes and each of them was difficult.

AFTERWARDS

My knowledge of the Korean language, and my experience with and knowledge about computers and library technology was a good match with SNU's needs. Any change or any project I did was new to them, and each one made a positive contribution in different areas. I truly felt that every work day was exciting (mostly 9:00 a.m. to 5:00 p.m. Monday through Friday; I opted not to work on Saturdays even though the Korean work force still work a half day on Saturday). I was eager to share and teach my experiences and knowledge to them.

The SNU personnel were considerate, and constantly asked about my needs, be it computer hardware, software, or office supplies, and best of all, delivered the requested items to me within days. The committee members were also eager to work hard and learn, were fully cooperative, and showed a true team spirit.

There were many areas in the law library that needed major changes and improvements: automated systems, budget, serials, acquisitions, collection, classification arrangement, reference services, and staff, but there are such strict limitations that making any major changes will take a long time.

One of the notable experiences I had was working with the computer lab graduate assistant. He was extremely knowledgeable about both hardware and software and was so dedicated and eager to learn new things that sometimes he even stayed late at night to finish projects, and, most of all, showed such respect, and appreciation. I learned a number of new things from him–Korean word processing, PowerPoint, and many useful tips in using computers.

I maintain contacts through e-mail messages with those faculty members who sat through my training sessions. The SIU law library has responded to a number of reference inquiries from Korea, and, in the fall of 1999, our law school hosted a visiting scholar from the SNU College of Law. From my sabbatical, a link has been established that is valuable to both schools.

In conclusion, I would like offer a bit of advice for those who are considering work in a foreign library. The foremost quality that you need is to be flexible. No matter how well you organize and plan before your departure, there is always the unexpected, and you need to be able to make changes and adapt quickly. The next is to be an expert as much as you can in all areas of library management, not just your specific area. You will need to be a resource person for many questions from diverse groups. Knowledge in searching and finding online and Internet resources is also a must, and skills in HTML page design and the use of word processing, spreadsheet, database, and presentation software will also be very useful. Having a helpful attitude of "May I help you?," "Do you want me to show you this?," or "I can do this for you" will not only develop close personal contacts, but also will build a successful and pleasant working environment. There is one thing that it is completely beyond your control: dealing with government bureaucracy for work/research permits, visas, etc. Based on my experience, you should calculate the time to take at least two or three times longer than you would normally expect.

I truly appreciate the spirit of a sabbatical leave that allowed me to have this opportunity and cherish the experience and personal contacts. It was mutually beneficial; moreover, it truly rejuvenated my work and enriched my knowledge.

NOTES

1. Sang-Hyun Song, *Korean Law in the Global Economy* 338 (1996).

2. A Pentium computer!–our law school at that time didn't own any Pentiums, and I was still using a 486 machine at SIU in 1997.

3. The URL for the SNU College of Law home page is http://law.snu.ac.kr/ (last visited Sept. 25, 2000).

4. *Index of Korean Legal Literature* (Seoul National University Press, 1978-1996). Volume 1 covers 1945-1974, vol. 2, 1975-1985, vol. 3, 1986-1992 and volume 4, 1993-1995. The database for this index is available from the SNU library home page at: http://solarsnet.snu.ac.kr/law/law.htm (last visited Sept. 25, 2000).

Law School on the Liffey: My Experiences at Trinity College, Dublin

Janet Sinder

SUMMARY. In 1996, the author lived in Dublin, Ireland, while researching Irish legal history. During that time, she developed a relationship with the Law School at Trinity College, Dublin which has allowed her to return there to work on the Law School's Web site and to teach online legal research to the students and staff. In addition to discussing her experiences, the author provides basic advice for living and working overseas. *[Article copies available for a fee from The Haworth Document Delivery Service: 1-800-342-9678. E-mail address: <getinfo@haworthpressinc.com> Website: <http://www.HaworthPress.com> © 2000 by The Haworth Press, Inc. All rights reserved.]*

In 1996, I was lucky to be able to spend four months in Dublin, Ireland, researching Irish legal history. Since then, I've been invited back four times to the Trinity College, Dublin School of Law, each time for about ten days.

My first trip to Dublin was possible because all librarians at the Duke Law Library with Continuing Appointment (our University Libraries' version of tenure) are entitled to request up to four months of release time for a special project. I became interested in Irish legal history a number of years ago after editing a bibliography on the subject for *Law Library Journal.*[1] I decided to request release time to write an article about the sources for researching Irish legal history.

Janet Sinder is Head of Information Services, Duke University School of Law Library.

[Haworth co-indexing entry note]: "Law School on the Liffey: My Experiences at Trinity College, Dublin." Sinder, Janet. Co-published simultaneously in *Legal Reference Services Quarterly* (The Haworth Information Press, an imprint of The Haworth Press, Inc.) Vol. 18, No. 3, 2000, pp. 101-109; and: *Law Librarians Abroad* (ed: Janet Sinder) The Haworth Information Press, an imprint of The Haworth Press, Inc., 2000, pp. 101-109. Single or multiple copies of this article are available for a fee from The Haworth Document Delivery Service [1-800-342-9678, 9:00 a.m. - 5:00 p.m. (EST). E-mail address: getinfo@haworthpressinc.com].

The only libraries in Ireland that will support extensive research in law and history are in Dublin, so the choice of which city to visit was clear.

My first step was to write to the law schools at Trinity College, Dublin and University College Dublin, enquiring about the possibility of becoming a visiting scholar; unfortunately, neither school has this type of program. The head of the Law Department at Trinity (law is an undergraduate degree in Ireland, as it is in the United Kingdom and elsewhere) did offer me some unofficial connection with the law school, the opportunity to give a talk to the faculty, and even to put me up in the Trinity Guest Rooms for my first few nights in Dublin. This, combined with its more central location in the city, made my choice to work at Trinity an easy one. Both universities were willing to provide me with a "Reader's Ticket" to the library and an e-mail account.

During my four-month stay, I tried to become as involved as I could in the life of the Law School. I discovered that in Ireland the law school and the library are two entirely separate entities. There is no Law Library, as such, instead there is simply a law collection in the main university library. At Trinity, there is a librarian who devotes part of her time to law, but it is a far cry from the extensive law reference staff I was used to. Another shock to the system was how crowded the library is when students are studying. The first six weeks of my stay coincided with the time when students study for exams (held only once a year), and I was warned that although I would be given a Reader's Ticket for the library, this would not guarantee that I would find a seat.

Posted in the library are numerous signs warning that if you leave your seat for more than fifteen minutes, someone else is entitled to take it. While it was always easy to find a seat in the morning, I became very adept at buying and eating lunch in fifteen minutes so as not to lose my precious space. Space is so tight that many students study in chairs with desks attached, placed in front of the stacks, so that you had to ask them to move in order to retrieve a book. Fortunately, by mid-May the students began to leave, and for the rest of my stay, the library was virtually empty.

As mentioned by Nancy Carter in her article,[2] Trinity closes its library for two weeks each July. During that time, I worked at the National Library of Ireland, another interesting experience. To use the library, you must first apply. Once permission is granted (this happens right away–no waiting period), your photo is taken and you are given a laminated ID card. Each day, upon arriving at the library, you sign in, leave all your belongings except paper and pen in a locker with a guard (yes, even your purse must be locked up), and walk upstairs to the reading room. There, for every book or journal, you fill out a card and give it to the librarian. It is then retrieved by a page and brought to your desk. But while the workings of the National Library seemed to come from an earlier time, I did note that it was much more encouraging of the use of laptops in the library than was Trinity (Trinity's posted rules for laptop computers were dated 1993).

While I was welcomed to Dublin by the law faculty at Trinity, I had no real status at the university. This meant that I could not check out books from the library or use most of the facilities. However, the law librarian arranged for me to have an e-mail account (one of my most crucial acquisitions), and one of the law faculty wangled a membership for me in the Senior Common Room (for £8/month, you can have coffee, read the newspaper, chat with other members, and generally hang out in very opulent surroundings right in the center of the college; membership is open only to faculty and senior staff).

In spite of my lack of "official" status, I became a rather constant fixture in the law school. One reason was that the law school served for a while as my only point of contact with the world back home (it took six weeks to have a phone installed in my apartment) and a place to receive faxes. I would have been completely lost without this and my Trinity e-mail account in the days before Hotmail and Internet cafes.

Since I knew no-one in Dublin and was working independently, I had no real colleagues. I took every opportunity to become involved in various law school activities. One of the first was a conference on film making in Ireland, where I worked at the registration table. I also attended a lot of receptions during the summer and even judged moot court arguments. Several law schools hold summer programs at Trinity, and Trinity law faculty teach courses in these programs.

While I thoroughly enjoyed working at Trinity, I was surprised at the lack of resources in the law school and, in particular, at the almost complete non-use of technology. While the university had a Web site, the link to the law school sat inactive; the law school had not really thought much about developing one. A few of the faculty used Lexis, but it was expensive and limited. They had a Westlaw contract, but, at the time, it was useful only when they were interested in American materials.[3] Coming from Duke, I've been spoiled by our extensive access to technology, and am also aware of the uses to which it can be put. I was determined to bring the light of technology into the "darkness" of the law school.

THE TRINITY LAW SCHOOL WEB SITE

Naturally, before my four months were up, I had fallen in love with life in Dublin and was anxious to find a way to return, even for a short while. Over a farewell lunch with the head of the law school, William Binchy, I mentioned that I thought it was very important for the law school to have a Web site, even one without a great deal of content. I followed this with a suggestion that I could come back some time in the near future to help the school set up their site. At the time, I did not have a lot of experience with the Web, but I had supervised the beginnings of the Duke Web site and thought putting up relatively straightforward information about the school and its staff and courses would be feasible in a short period of time. Prof. Binchy agreed, and we later decided I would come to Trinity in mid-December after classes had ended at Duke.

I envisioned myself holding meetings with the staff and acting as a consultant, after which they would know what they wanted on their Web site and how it should be structured. They would then develop the contents of the site, perhaps with the help of a graduate student to do the coding. Alas, my naivete about the way things worked set me up for a rude awakening.

I arrived in Dublin about two weeks before Christmas and realized immediately that the Irish take the Christmas season, which includes all of December, extremely seriously. It is imperative to meet up for a drink with everyone you've ever known; there was little time to think about "virtual" matters like Web sites. After several days at the law school, with not much to do, I was given some material to put on the Web. So much for my vision of myself as the consultant bringing together the great ideas of others into an expression of the spirit of the law school. Instead, I designed some simple Web pages and typed in and coded the material myself.

While the visit turned out very differently from what I had imagined, several good things resulted from it: the Web site was up and running before I left, and I had talked myself into another trip back to Dublin within the year, this time to do something I was more suited for–training students and staff to use Lexis and Westlaw. It also taught me yet another lesson in trying to make the best of any situation: It was better to create a simple Web site than to leave Dublin with no Web site at all. I was also able to train someone at the law school to make changes on the site after I left.

Though it might be thought that anyone at Trinity could have done what I did, in a law school where the small staff is very busy, and no one has free time for additional projects, it sometimes takes an outsider to come in and get a project off the ground. Not only did I create the Web pages, but I also had to spend hours sitting in the offices at Information Services, get access to the server, learn how to put files on the server, and download front end software for law school staff to use (at the time, I was using AOL Press, which was free, but took a long time to download over the Internet).

The Trinity law school Web site remains in existence; I redesigned it in the autumn of 1998. All of the changes this time were made via FTP, from North Carolina. The staff at the law school would like to maintain the site themselves, but they are already overwhelmed with their regular business, and their technological resources also make it more difficult.

If you do find yourself in the position of creating or maintaining a Web site for another organization, make sure it's simple. The site should be set up so that someone without much experience or equipment can easily take it over. This means minimizing the use of graphics that will have to be changed. Since updating will be a problem, design a site that is not very time-specific, but that includes mainly general information. Don't assume that people in that organization will be able to use "simple" front end software to maintain the site. This software may be too expensive, and it usually does not run well on low end machines.

LEXIS AND WESTLAW TRAINING

After my Web experience, I was happy to return to Trinity to do something for which I was far better trained. Since 1997, I've visited the law school each October to teach classes in Lexis and Westlaw. I go to Dublin for a week while Duke is on Fall break, and each year I've done a bit more teaching than the year before. In addition to Lexis and Westlaw, I've taught a few classes in legal research on the Internet, although that is becoming less necessary. Students are more familiar with Web searching, and I can simply give them a handout of good sites for legal research.

The first two years I taught only the LL.M. students and staff; this past year I also taught classes on Lexis to undergraduates. Trinity began an LL.M. program in the autumn of 1997. It attracts many Irish students and some students from Europe, Australia, and even the U.S. It is a one year program similar to the LL.M. programs U.S. schools have for foreign students, although students specialize in a particular subject and are taught separately from the undergraduates. The undergraduate students are more like our law students, although they begin at a younger age. The law degree is a four year program at Trinity, and a three year program at other Irish universities

One thing my time at Trinity has taught me is to be completely flexible in how I teach. At one time or other, I've done the following: (1) taught in a computer lab where the students could use the computers and my computer was projected on a screen; (2) taught small groups of students at two terminals that, if we were lucky, would both have access to Lexis/Westlaw at the same time; and (3) taught Lexis in a lecture format where the students could see a projected computer screen, but would never have any hands-on training.

The use of Lexis and Westlaw in Ireland is completely different from what I am used to. It is only in the past few years, when Westlaw decided to enter the European market, that the law school has received any kind of price break on a searching contract. At the present time, the school has one Westlaw password for students, which is used only by the post-graduate students. Trinity now has a Lexis contract that provides individual passwords for all of its law students and for the teaching staff. Two terminals are located in the library, and the LL.M. students have two terminals they can use in their student lounge. These two computers are for Lexis, Westlaw, the Web, and e-mail, and are connected to the university's network.

The use of computers for research is not ingrained in the students the way that it is in the U.S. Therefore, the students are less anxious to learn about Lexis and Westlaw. They do not use it for job searches, and it is more difficult to explain to them why they would want to use it. Whereas in the U.S. I would expect almost every student to turn up at a class where they could learn to search online, in Dublin only a small proportion did.

ADVICE FOR WORKING OVERSEAS

My first piece of advice would be, if you want to do something, ask for it, and be persistent (but not annoying). I would never have gotten the opportunity to work at Trinity if I hadn't convinced the head of the law school that I could provide something they needed (even if they didn't realize beforehand that they needed it). Although there are certainly other people in Ireland who could have created the law school's Web site, or who could come in to teach Lexis and Westlaw, no one else offered to do it. Convince the people in charge that you will be able to save them work.

Be flexible (I think all of the articles in this text offer the same piece of advice). I am by nature an inveterate planner, but when dealing with life overseas, I try to go with the flow as much as possible and to accept that everything will indeed work out in the end. Each year I'm a nervous wreck because my departure is only weeks away, and I still don't know how or what I'm going to be teaching. In 1999, I discovered ten days in advance that I would be lecturing on Lexis to the undergraduates, something I'd never done before, and I was asked to prepare a four-page handout for them. I was told that I would be able to demonstrate Lexis on a computer in the lecture hall, but previous experience told me to bring overheads with screen shots as a backup in case the Internet connection failed. (I was pleasantly surprised that the classroom computer was probably the best one I worked on anywhere in Ireland, and the Internet connection worked perfectly.)

This was a contrast to the previous year when the two computers for the LL.M.s were hooked up to the Internet approximately 5 minutes before the first training session was scheduled to begin. The building we were in was under renovation at the time, and the computer lines were temporary. Fortunately, I was the only one who seemed at all panicked by the situation.

I've also had to allow a lot of time to get things organized once I arrive. Don't assume that things will be done in advance, because the people you've asked to do them probably don't have time, and they certainly don't have that much motivation to do things until you are there in person asking about them.

Assume that the resources anywhere you go will not be as good as they are in the U.S. and that everything will be done differently. When I taught Lexis and Westlaw in a computer lab in 1997, I had to sit with someone from the university's I.S. department while they loaded the software onto the network for that classroom and also had to arrange for telnet access for the lab to be turned on just for the few hours I was teaching (most undergraduates at Trinity do not have access to the Web outside the university's site unless a faculty member approves their request for it, and telnet access is turned off for all the public computer labs). While everything worked out in the end, it involved numerous phone calls to arrange everything and hours spent waiting for someone to have time to work on the problem. It's worth the time and effort to be as nice as possible to all I.T. personnel; they are always very busy, and you are creating even more work for them.

Teaching overseas also involves knowing how the educational system works and what the students will need to do. Students in Ireland do much less research than American students, and they do not work on law journals. Therefore, it required some thinking and asking around to decide what aspects of online research would be meaningful to them.

LIVING IN A FOREIGN LAND

Apart from work life being exceedingly different, living in another country really is a foreign experience. Even a country that seems as much like the U.S. as Ireland does (they speak English, don't they?) is completely different. Some chores were very easy (getting a library card at the public library, opening a bank account), and some were truly eye-opening (getting a telephone where no phone lines had been run to a brand-new apartment building in the center of the city; dealing with the police after being burglarized).

Spend as much time as you can preparing before you go. You don't want to spend your time overseas worrying about things at home. While it's not mandatory that you open a foreign bank account (you can get all the money you need via an ATM), I found it very helpful. If you have to pay utilities, you can have them direct debited rather than leaving a deposit. It's also an easy way to deal with any checks you may receive in foreign currency. And at the end of your stay, most banks should be able to give you your balance in a check made out in dollars.

Determined to live as much as possible like a native on my first trip, I began looking for an apartment as soon as I arrived in Dublin. It's not always easy to find a short term lease, and I discovered that offering to pay slightly more than the asking price for rent opened up many more possibilities. I could hardly believe that I would be "bargaining" to pay more than the asking price, but living overseas is stressful enough. It's worth spending a bit more to make life a little easier. And while I had joked before leaving about the hovel I'd be living in, coming face-to-face with some real Dublin basement flats made me realize that was not the life I was cut out for. Experiences such as this are a reason to have a cushion of money to rely on when overseas.

Go out on your own and meet people, even if you'd never do that in the U.S. If you're cautious at first, go to tourist locations and talk to other Americans. They're sure to be envious that you're living there, while they're only visiting, and will want to know everything about life in another country. After you've mastered the art of talking to your compatriots, you can move on to the locals.

Keep in touch after you leave. This is simple to do with the advent of e-mail. You never know when the opportunity will arise for you to return, and it's wonderful to have friends in another country.

Finally, be prepared to enjoy yourself. One way to make yourself see disasters in a humorous light is to write about them. I sent an e-mail letter back to my library every week and tried to turn all of my frustrations with the way things worked into anecdotes. Now I can read those e-mails (which someone collected in a notebook for me on my return) and enjoy only good memories of my experience.

NOTES

1. *See* Barbara Pawloski, *Gaelic Law in Early and Medieval Ireland: A Bibliography*, 79 Law Libr. J. 305 (1987).

2. *See* Nancy Carol Carter, *Law School Abroad: Ghiberti to Guinness*, Legal Ref. Serv. Q., Vol. 18, No. 3, 2000, at 15.

3. Westlaw has just added a number of UK case databases, the most comprehensive of which is UK-RPTS-ALL. Westlaw also offers access to the *Legal Journals Index*, the comprehensive index for UK and Irish journals in the LJI database.

A Down Under Reference Experience

William Smith

SUMMARY. In the summer of 1999, the author, a library science student pursuing his master's degree at the University of North Carolina at Chapel Hill, travelled to Australia to do a field experience at the University of Sydney Law Library. This article talks about his experience, discussing, among other issues, his experiences behind the reference desk and difficulties in learning how to research Australian law. *[Article copies available for a fee from The Haworth Document Delivery Service: 1-800-342-9678. E-mail address: <getinfo@haworthpressinc.com> Website: <http://www.HaworthPress.com> © 2000 by The Haworth Press, Inc. All rights reserved.]*

In the summer of 1999, I travelled to Australia. Though the primary purpose of my trip was to dive the Great Barrier Reef and explore the great island continent before the Olympics, I also was fortunate to have the opportunity to spend some time at the University of Sydney Faculty of Law's library. Guided by the "work hard, play hard" principle, I first went to the law library for my g'day mate reference experience, saving my visit with the koalas and kangaroos for later in my trip.

And now a commercial advertisement: This Australian experience was made possible by a number of generous individuals, not the least of whom were Margaret McAlese, the Law Librarian at the University of Sydney Faculty of Law, who allowed me to practice my reference skills on her down under patrons in exchange for my teaching Westlaw

---

William Smith is Reference Librarian, University of Southern California Law Library.

[Haworth co-indexing entry note]: "A Down Under Reference Experience." Smith, William. Co-published simultaneously in *Legal Reference Services Quarterly* (The Haworth Information Press, an imprint of The Haworth Press, Inc.) Vol. 18, No. 3, 2000, pp. 111-118; and: *Law Librarians Abroad* (ed: Janet Sinder) The Haworth Information Press, an imprint of The Haworth Press, Inc., 2000, pp. 111-118. Single or multiple copies of this article are available for a fee from The Haworth Document Delivery Service [1-800-342-9678, 9:00 a.m. - 5:00 p.m. (EST). E-mail address: getinfo@haworthpressinc.com].

to certain members of the library staff and evaluating/weeding the library's American collection; and James B. Perrine, a law school colleague of mine, J.S.D. candidate at Yale Law School and Fulbright Scholar currently visiting the University of Sydney Faculty of Law, who kindly provided me with accommodation for the duration of my stay in Sydney. I also must extend a note of thanks to David Partlett, Professor of Law, Vanderbilt University Law School, and Dick Danner, Senior Associate Dean for Library and Computing, Duke University School of Law, for supporting and furthering my efforts to work in Australia by contacting Margaret McAlese on my behalf. Finally, my gratitude must be extended to the administration at the Duke University Law School Library for graciously replying "no worries" when I asked them whether I could pursue a once in a lifetime opportunity without fearing the loss of gainful employment.

In my view, the culmination of an educational pursuit is not reached until the student is provided a means to implement the theory learned in the classroom through practical experience in a real world atmosphere. The School of Information and Library Science at the University of North Carolina in Chapel Hill provides its students such educational opportunities through field experiences. Field experiences are "designed to provide the student with the opportunity to work in a day-to-day professional environment under the supervision of an experienced librarian or information specialist."[1] The field experience guidelines require a student to design a specific set of goals and objectives to be accomplished, complete a minimum of 115 hours of work at the site location, and file periodic reports about progress made towards the established objectives. Upon completion of the field experience, the student must write a final paper describing and analyzing the overall experience.

For some reason, my faculty advisor did not agree that simply traveling abroad and exploring the Australian Outback were sufficient objectives to satisfy the requirements for a field experience and earn three credit hours towards my M.L.S. degree. Part of her objection stemmed from my suggestion that I become the protégé of a professional tour guide instead of an Australian information professional. Thus, I capitulated to my advisor's demands and resolved to "tour" the University of Sydney Faculty of Law's library. My goals for the field experience were to develop an understanding of the basic principles of Australian legal research, compare some general aspects of

American and Australian law libraries, and compare reference experiences in the University of Sydney Law Library with those I have had at the Duke University School of Law Library.

Under the theory that providing reference service at an Australian law library would be the best means to accomplish each of my objectives, I boarded a plane for Sydney in May 1999. Less than 48 hours after my arrival and while still recovering from jet lag, I found myself behind the reference desk at the University of Sydney Law Library. After receiving a ten minute introduction to the library collection, the extent of my preparation to field my first reference question in Australia, I was wondering how quickly the library patrons would seek my assistance. Not surprisingly, I quickly noticed that Murphy's law transcends hemispheres. That day, the computing system in the law library was inoperable, having crashed the previous Saturday at 2:15 in the afternoon. There was no access to the online catalog or any materials outside the law school. Needless to say, at that point, the theory I had learned in the classroom was my security blanket.

I had been working the reference desk all of fifteen minutes when a patron approached and asked a question about finding prior amendments to an Australian statute. I expected my new colleague, Ross Dickinson, who is the Shelving Supervisor at the Library and, like all employees at the Library, spends a fair amount of time staffing a combined reference and circulation desk, to field the question. Ross, however, quickly explained to the patron that the location of the Australian statutes in the library would be the extent of his knowledge. Unaware that I had literally been in the library no more than 30 minutes and that I did not even know the location of the statutes in the library, the patron turned to me. It did not help that my new colleague decided to point out to the patron that I was, among other things, a library science student and law graduate. After briefly explaining my "American heritage," I walked over to the statutes with the patron, trusting that the prior amendments to the Australian statute would be noted at the end of the current statute, as they are in American legislation. Fortunately, my presumption was correct, and I was greeted with reference success. From that point onwards, until the day I departed, I was that particular patron's favorite librarian, at least when she had a reference question.

My initial reference success contrasted with the obstacles I would have to overcome to accomplish my primary objective of developing an understanding of the basic principles of Australian legal research. This, in fact, proved to be my most difficult task. The problems ranged from a lack of guidance in the library, undeveloped electronic databases, and inadequate paper resources, at least in comparison to the sources I had been accustomed to in the United States. First, the legal research professors did not work in the library, and only three members of the library staff, including the Law Librarian, had received extensive legal research training. Thus, part of my effort included meeting with the legal research professors, attending legal research classes, and reading research guides. In each one of these experiences, I found that there was a heavy reliance on secondary sources, particularly in the initial stages of the research process, not dissimilar to the process in the United States.

The research difficulties really started to materialize when the focus shifted to retrieving cases or statutes online through AGIS (Attorney General's Information Service) and AUSTLII (Australian Legal Information Institute), two of the major legal databases relied on by the University of Sydney Law Library, without having a specific case or statute to direct the search. This gave rise to the second obstacle to my research objective: researching specific subject areas proved to be all but impossible, unless you had a few hours. This difficulty arose because the electronic databases were underdeveloped, in that only limited Boolean searching was allowed (i.e., only the "and," "or," and "not" connectors were functional). Additionally, the databases were not narrowly defined, compared to those in Westlaw and Lexis. Although it is possible to limit searches to a specific database, because of the nature of Internet searches and the wealth of material available in the database, a number of irrelevant hits is usually generated.

Unfortunately, the third obstacle to achieving my objectives was that even these less than satisfactory electronic searches were better than attempting to search only with paper resources (e.g., indexes or digests). The only reason I could find for the inadequacy of paper resources was a lack of competition between publishers and vendors in Australia. Although there is an Australian monthly digest, its coverage is selective and inconsistent in some subject areas. Not all of the cases released by the court are included in the digest, and the selection process is not limited to leading cases. Therefore, the digest is not widely used for research. Additionally, there is no topic and key number system to assist you in navigating the subject areas. For instance, in the latest West Digest, under the subject Physicians and Surgeons, you will find close to 130 subdivisions. In Australia, on the other hand, there are no such subdivisions. Thus I found that secondary sources presented the best approach to researching Australian law. To the credit of the library staff, even with these obstacles, they appeared to meet the needs of the patrons they were serving.

Since language is a key instrument in the process of communicating, and English is not only the most common language in Australia, but also the native language of most Australians, language barriers should not have been an obstacle. I had expected to run into accent problems, but linguistic problems had never crossed my mind. The best example of a language obstacle occurred when a patron approached to borrow a pen. The patron had a broad southern Australian accent. Of course, again affirming the global nature of Murphy's law, I was working the desk alone when he approached and said: "Can I borrow a biro?" To me, it sounded like: "Can I borrow a borrow?" After I responded that I did not understand, the patron became visibly upset and posited his question again in a raised voice. Fortunately, a kind student behind the patron informed me that he intended to borrow a pen. Thus, my field experience presented some very unexpected cultural challenges in addition to the research difficulties that I was anticipating.

One of the first things I gained from my reference experience at the University of Sydney Law Library is a greater appreciation of the wealth of resources that are so easily accessible from the network at the Duke Law Library. Though the resources at the University of Sydney are considerable, they are outmatched by those available at a major American law school.

My reference experience in Sydney highlighted other differences between working in an Australian and American law libraries apart from the expected legal and somewhat unexpected linguistic dissimilarities I mentioned above. As mentioned earlier, the law library at the University of Sydney has a combined reference/circulation desk, while an American law library generally has a separate desk for each task. The multi-task demands of the combined desk in Sydney presented an environment different from the familiar environs of the distinct reference desk I staff at Duke. Although the increased patron contact associated with a combined desk provided a welcome diversion from the sometimes inactive reference desk, particularly during the exam season or the early morning or late evening shift, certain aspects of the combined desk were not as enjoyable. While common circulation duties, such as checking out and checking in books, were not bothersome, attempting to repair jammed copy machines and crashing computers was a less than stimulating chore.

That only one service point was available in the law library also meant that all library staff were involved in reference service. While this proved to be helpful when large numbers of students were simultaneously borrowing books and seeking directional information, I found it to be detrimental in those instances where a patron had a specific legal inquiry. Often in those instances, the patron's inquiry was beyond the knowledge of the service provider, since many of the library staff members did not have any special legal research training or an extensive legal background. Although having law librarians with J.D. and M.L.S. degrees does not always assure reference success, I would argue that it certainly enhances the possibilities of more fully meeting the needs of the patrons.

Another benefit the dual service point approach provides, in addition to providing companionship that, in my experience, has generally not been available in a law school reference desk setting in the United States, is the complementary skills of reference and circulation specialists in one setting. Finally, the dual desk promotes collegial camaraderie shown by the somewhat tempered, but, nonetheless, invigorating debates I experienced in Sydney about the entertainment value of NFL football as compared to rugby or nine innings of major league baseball as compared to five days of Test cricket. Though I can testify that I had these conversations while I was working in Sydney, I shall not reveal my position on these important issues of international affairs.

In comparing American and Australian law libraries, three other issues came to the forefront: distance learning, labor organizations, and hours of operation. An unusual part of the Australian University experience is distance learning, a direct function of the tremendous size and relatively sparse population of the country. Some students, though attending the University of Sydney, actually live in the Outback. To support the students who live outside the metropolitan area with library services, the library practiced what I will characterize as "distance lending." Distance lending was designed to allow the library to provide services to meet the needs of the various curricula throughout the university community, and I witnessed the benefits of this program to a specific group of law library patrons, *Legal Practitioners Admission Board* (LPAB) students. Some LPAB students reside in the "country" (i.e., outside the Sydney metroplex) and obtain legal credentials via non-traditional means, primarily through correspondence. Under the law library's "Country Lending" scheme, a part of the distance lending program, LPAB students can request, by e-mail, telephone, or facsimile, material to be delivered via post. The loan period for "Country Lending" items is a week longer than the period for regular circulation materials.

Though the participants undoubtedly viewed the situation differently, I was also fortunate to gain a unique perspective on industrial relations in an Australian law library during my time in Sydney. I was unaware, upon my arrival, that law faculty members and law library staff are part of organized labor. While I was completing my field experience work at the law library, the union for the law faculty, frustrated with actions taken by the administration in eliminating certain positions when individuals retired, threatened a strike. Though the strike never came to fruition–it was called off on a last minute vote by leaders of the union–watching the events unfold was very interesting. The mechanisms of carrying out a strike were similar to those that I had seen in the United States (e.g., picketing, carrying placards, and refusing to work), but the nature of the strike was very different. Rather than walking out until their demands were met through the negotiation process, the strikes were more symbolic in nature, in that the strike lasted only half a day. Though not an expert in Australian industrial relations matters, I questioned the effectiveness of such a limited strike, given that it was planned for morning operating hours, instead of the afternoon, when most patrons frequent the library, and was only a one-day affair. Fortunately for me, since a strike would have delayed my fulfilling the requirements for my field experience and my trip to the Outback, the industrial relations dispute only added positives, no negatives, to my stay in Sydney.

Unlike most law schools in the United States, the law library at the University of Sydney did not offer its patrons extended hours to the library collection and services. Generally, the hours of operation were 8:30 a.m. to 9:00 p.m. The library hours were not extended during exam periods, and neither students nor faculty were provided with twenty-four hour access. These limited hours may be attributed to the fact that union employees were only permitted to work thirty-five hours per week. Though I felt some pressure not to work over the thirty-five hour workweek, I decided it was necessary to do so in order to maximize my learning experience. Without question, those extended hours proved to be beneficial in helping me meet all my objectives prior to the conclusion of my field experience.

After successfully completing the requirements for the field experience, I felt it appropriate to make a personal reference inquiry, not at the law library, but at the nearest travel agency. And fortunately and hopefully, like so many of my down under patrons, I too was greeted with reference success. As I walked away from the desk in the travel agency the with tickets in hand, having been more than pleased with the reference interview process and the discount tickets, I knew that it was truly time to discover Australia. You can measure the number of credits I received towards my masters degree at the University of North Carolina at Chapel Hill and the number of hours I spent behind the reference desk at the University of Sydney's Law Library, but you cannot measure the value of my Australian experience. With my apologies to MasterCard, it was priceless.

NOTE

1. School of Information and Library Science, *Professional Field Experience: Program Philosophy*, *at* http://ils.unc.edu/field/philos.htm (last visited Dec. 15, 1999).

Assisting with Information Technology in East Africa

William W. Wells, Jr.

SUMMARY. There are opportunities for Law Librarians, no matter what their position, to assist with the development of information technology in many interesting locations throughout the world. This article describes two such opportunities experienced by the author in East Africa. The article also provides a starting place for those who wish to become involved as well as listing some issues one should take into consideration when considering such an opportunity. *[Article copies available for a fee from The Haworth Document Delivery Service: 1-800-342-9678. E-mail address: <getinfo@haworthpressinc.com> Website: <http://www.HaworthPress.com> © 2000 by The Haworth Press, Inc. All rights reserved.]*

INTRODUCTION

Between 1995 and 1999, I was fortunate enough to be twice asked to come to a country in Africa to assist them with their planning and use of information technology. In July 1995, I was invited to Asmara, Eritrea, to work with the University of Asmara. In September 1999, I was asked to go to Kampala, Uganda, to serve as a visiting scholar/consultant. Both of these invitations arrived in an unexpected manner, took a long time to be fleshed out, and then, because of budgetary considerations, became urgent. From my perspective, this seems to be

William W. Wells, Jr. is Law Library Director and Professor of Law, University of Maine School of Law, and Associate Provost for Technology, Information Systems and Libraries, University of Southern Maine.

[Haworth co-indexing entry note]: "Assisting with Information Technology in East Africa." Wells, Jr., William W. Co-published simultaneously in *Legal Reference Services Quarterly* (The Haworth Information Press, an imprint of The Haworth Press, Inc.) Vol. 18, No. 3, 2000, pp. 119-130; and: *Law Librarians Abroad* (ed: Janet Sinder) The Haworth Information Press, an imprint of The Haworth Press, Inc., 2000, pp. 119-130. Single or multiple copies of this article are available for a fee from The Haworth Document Delivery Service [1-800-342-9678, 9:00 a.m. - 5:00 p.m. (EST). E-mail address: getinfo@haworthpressinc.com].

the typical method of doing things when dealing with the projects primarily funded by our government.

My trips were sponsored by the United States Agency for International Development (USAID)[1] and the United States Information Agency (USIA)[2] and, as a result, each had a different underlying theme and focus. The majority of the United States' nonmilitary aid is funneled through USAID. It typically funds projects that aid in the economic development of the country. An example of this funding is the construction of dams in flood-prone areas of Africa. Its projects tend to be focused and result-oriented–there has to be a demonstrated "thing" accomplished.

Due to a much smaller funding base, USIA projects tend to be somewhat less grand in monetary scale and are nominally intended to be related to the promotion of democracy, education, and information about the United States–arguably much more grand and ambitious than a dam construction project. It is interesting, and quite ironic, that the programs with the longest term goals and the greatest potential to provide the most stability for these countries are funded at such a modest level. Two of the best known programs sponsored by USIA are the Fulbright and Humphrey fellowship programs. On the other hand, programs focused almost entirely upon quick economic gains seem to be funded quite generously. The differing purposes of my visits to Eritrea and Uganda are illustrative of these two diverse methods of assistance.

WHAT I DID

Eritrea

Initially, I was asked to go to Eritrea to consult on library automation. Specifically, the University of Asmara was interested in automating their catalog and related services, and I was asked to come to the University, review the collection, physical plant, and educational program, and make a recommendation as to what they should consider doing.

The first question that enters the mind of anyone who hears about someone making this type of trip is "why did they ask him?" There are a couple of answers to this that are probably typical of many situations. First, I have had experience in the automation of two law libraries. The first was the George Washington University Jacob Burns Law Library. This was a stand-alone automation project accomplished in 1984-1985. The second project was a much larger and complicated project in Maine. Beginning in 1989 and continuing today in another guise, the University of Maine system automated and integrated the eight separate libraries of its seven campuses–the University of Maine Garbrecht Law Library was one of these libraries. The fact that I had been working in law libraries was not a major factor. They did not have a need for a law librarian for my project. What they needed was a librarian who had experience in library automation, and I happened to be such an individual.

The second reason I was chosen resulted from the phenomenon of distance placing a halo on the consultant. Essentially, this means that the further a consultant travels to a site, the more authority that consultant's recommendations seem to carry. Having acknowledged this fact, it was this unfortunate devaluation of local talent in library and university circles which allowed me to have two extraordinary experiences.

Before I agreed to go to Eritrea, I wanted to make sure that I was not placing myself in a situation where I would fail. This led to a series of early morning telephone calls between the President of the University of Asmara and myself. We both had to be comfortable with the knowledge that we knew exactly what the University wanted done and what outcome was expected, and we also needed to resolve compensation issues. We agreed that the purpose of my visit was as stated above–to come look at their library and make a recommendation for automating its operations. As a result, I agreed to come, the travel arrangements were made for me, and I departed within three weeks of the agreement.

When I arrived, I had an initial briefing by the University Librarian and the President of the University. This briefing resulted in the expansion of my duties to include reviewing the University's administrative functions for possible automation.[3] At the end of the briefing, I was left to accomplish my duties.

Both of my projects were accomplished using the same methodology. This involved interviewing each person in the library and the administrative offices. In the library, I had to ascertain what the current staffing was and what it was accomplishing. This was done for several reasons. The first was to evaluate the collection and the facilities that housed the library. The second purpose was to determine the level of professionalism and training of the staff. Finally, I wanted to try to gauge the level of willingness to accept the changes automation would entail. As it turned out, this plan of attack was the correct one.

Although the President of the University, the Librarian, and I understood why I was there, no one had bothered to inform the library staff of the reasons for my visit. As a result, I had the task of explaining to each person, individually, the "real" reason for my presence. The concept of automation was received with a certain amount of concern and doubt (not unlike the feelings of the staff in my two previous automation experiences). This placed me in the position of counselor and educator as well as the consultant. I had to explain to each section of the library how automation would change their jobs.

The main staff concerns were typical for any library. Essentially, they were concerned about the lack of paper backup and that they would lose control over their area. Information is power. For those of you who have an integrated library system, try to recall the days prior to automation. The order records were the domain of acquisitions. Serials staff controlled all information about receipt of issues. Circulation controlled any association of patron to circulating materials. But, in the integrated system, everyone potentially has access to all of this information. This was a big change for us in the two libraries I helped automate, and it naturally loomed as a large one for the Eritreans.

I followed a similar procedure when I met with the administrative areas of the University: Admissions, Student Records, Purchasing, and Business Office. Their concerns were similar: How would the necessary redundancy be built in? How secure would the records be? Why would the University want to integrate these functions? How would this affect my job? Would I still have a job? Through the interview procedure I was able to provide enough information to help these individuals understand how these changes would work, as well as successfully gain a picture of their current procedures. I was not completely successful in getting them all to accept the necessity of these changes up front.

After all of the interviews, I had to synthesize the information into an understandable and coherent explanation of the current situation and then propose a workable recommendation for the automation of the Library and the administrative functions of the University. My recommendations were given in a written report proposing a specific library system for purchase, as well as suggesting ways to begin automating the administrative functions of the University.

I would like to be able to say that all of my recommendations were followed and that the University was happy with the design of the systems. However, progress in this area was, and is, slow. Six months after I left, the University did decide to acquire the automated library system, but they needed an aid package to fund it. Unfortunately, the aid did not come as fast as anticipated, and, tragically, since February 1998, Eritrea has been at war with Ethiopia and almost all available resources are going to support this effort.[4]

Uganda

Initially, I was asked to go to Uganda to discuss the use of information technology as a means of providing access to legal information to a greater number of people. However, as things progressed my role was expanded somewhat–away from specifically legal information toward access to all types of information and ways this access could encourage the growth of democracy. The reason for the expansion of my role came from USIA's understanding of my background.

In addition to my role as the Director of the Law Library at the University of Maine School of Law, I also serve as Associate Provost[5] at my parent institution. In my Associate Provost role, I am responsible for all the University of Southern Maine's networking, software support, distance education, and instructional support and libraries. This breadth of responsibility prompted the change in my programmed itinerary for Uganda.

Unlike my task in Eritrea, which was to recommend a specific product as well as a course of action, my role in Uganda was more to discuss, observe, and encourage the things I saw that had potential or were working well. To this end, I was fortunate to be asked to make three presentations and to meet with a variety of individuals, groups, and organizations.[6] Each group had their own particular areas of expertise as well as needs that seemed overwhelming to them. However, when one stepped back and looked at each of the strengths as part of a whole, there were a large core of good projects and strong individuals that could serve the country well.

My task was an interesting one from an international relations perspective. I was there as the guest of USIS and not the Ugandan government; therefore, my task was to serve more as a teacher and much less as an outside consultant who was going to "set things right." As a visiting outsider, I was able to see what each group was doing and how each piece could fit together. After gaining this insight, my "teaching" theme quickly became that the sharing of resources would spread the labor and become a benefit to all.

Uganda is a small country which also has a tragic recent history.[7] As a result, it is just beginning its journey to join the democratic countries of the world. Ugandans are poor and, consequently, are quite guarded in announcing any resources they may have for fear of either losing them or, what is worse, losing control of them.[8]

A brief recitation of the existing resources and projects will demonstrate why I emphasized sharing as the best mode for them to follow. The Parliamentary Library was making an electronic version of their Hansard's;[9] the Supreme Court was interested in making their decisions available electronically;[10] the Law Revision Commission was using electronic databases in recodifying the statutes;[11] the Legal Informatics Center at Makerere University was creating a search program to apply against an existing electronic version of the statutes. These four projects would provide the basic legal information needed in a country that is trying to establish a democratic government.

The reader might wonder why there was an emphasis upon providing information in an electronic format. After all, Uganda is a part of the Third World that is lacking all or most of the traditional infrastructure one associates with being an electronic information society. While this belief is understandable, the reality in Uganda is vastly different. It is true that there is not a robust traditional wire telecommunications environment. However, the country is well served by some interesting new ventures. There are three cellular phone companies in the capital of Kampala. Even more surprising to the visitor are the eight cyber cafes in Kampala utilizing satellite communication technology. Add to this three major international projects to bring digital wireless communication technology to East Africa, and it is easy to see why electronic information technology is the way to go. By not having the traditional communications infrastructure, Uganda is in a unique situation of not having to adapt legacy systems in the new information age. Instead, it is positioned to leapfrog over, and possibly surpass, the developed world in this one area of development.

The real question is whether the various organizations will be able to work together to provide and share these information resources. To be honest, it is still an open question. When I left Kampala, there was great excitement about the possibilities. A copy of the Embassy TELEX report to Washington[12] indicates that the USIS (USIA) people in Kampala were pleased with the results of the trip. They report post-visit excitement from the locals about moving ahead. However, the final result of my visit will be weighed against the actions of the players over the next two to three years.

HOW TO GET INVOLVED IN A PROJECT LIKE THIS

As mentioned in the introduction, the portal I used for my two visits to East Africa was the largesse, if not direct invitation, of two United States government agencies–USAID and USIA. Both of these agencies have programs to provide assistance in developing countries of the world. Depending upon your interests and abilities, one may be more appropriate than another.

USAID generally funds development projects[13] in various parts of the world. This was the case for my visit to the University of Asmara in Eritrea. The University of Asmara worked in partnership with the University of North Carolina, Chapel Hill, to facilitate an extensive program to regenerate university level education in Eritrea.[14] The University of North Carolina received funds from various sources, including USAID, to enable it to work with the University of Asmara to regain what was lost during the long civil war. Part of the program has as its goal the growth of the University library and preparation for the use of information technology. I was identified as a possible consultant through the search process designed to achieve this goal.

USIA, as well as its successor sections in the Department of State, is generally interested in projects that promote cultural and educational institutions.[15] In the instance of my Ugandan visit, and other similar programs, I had to apply directly to the agency. This application provided my educational background, professional qualifications, and references. The agency reviewed my application and then passed it on to the Embassy people in Uganda to see if they would be satisfied with my application. Once they decided that I would be an acceptable visitor, we negotiated travel times and specified the duties required of me.

The formality of the process depends upon the project. There is an application procedure in which the applicant's qualifications are evaluated against the needs of the program. The Fulbright and Humphrey fellowship programs use these rather stringently. The applicants provide their qualifications, make a proposal, and identify specific outcomes. They are reviewed at many levels within the Agency before a selection is made. Finally, there has to be a match between the host educational institution and the applicant before the award of the fellowship.

In my case, however, it was somewhat more informal. To some extent the selection process was more an extension of an "old boys network" than normal. In both situations there was the need for someone to be selected in a relatively short period of time. I was called and asked if I would either be interested or knew someone who might be willing to do the project. In both instances, my going was not a foregone conclusion. I still had to provide a justification of my qualifications to the "host." Both the host and I had to be sure that this was something that I could accomplish, and I had to be sure this was something I was comfortable doing.

How does one get asked to do something like this? Outside of a certain amount of ego and a bit of luck, persistence is the best method. Make yourself known in circles of those doing things in which you wish to participate. Start applying to agencies for fellowships in the areas where you feel you can be of assistance. Go to meetings where these issues are the topic. Build up some personal contacts with those who have done this sort of thing in the past.[16] This is really no different than many of the interesting things one can do through AALL. Having the requisite educational and professional qualifications is mandatory; however, knowing someone who can recommend you is invaluable. The same is true for membership on the periodic ABA/AALS re-accreditation visiting teams for law schools in the United States and evaluation of United States law school sponsored programs in international sites. There is no coincidence that the same people are asked to do these tasks. These people are not the only ones qualified. They are, however, the people who have demonstrated they have the ability and have made an effort to ensure that it is known they are willing to participate.

WHAT TO KNOW ABOUT YOURSELF TO BE SUCCESSFUL

One's education, professional competency, and reputation can be easily evaluated, but the most important part of being successful in these situations is knowing yourself. What are your personal strengths and weaknesses? For us all this type of self-assessment can be quite enlightening and sobering.

Are you a person who is comfortable dealing with change and ambiguity? This may impact upon the eventual success of your participation in these programs. One can generally tell from the initial description of the project just how structured it is. I found this to be true in both of my projects. It was clear from the outset that conditions, needs, and desires were changing after each preliminary conversation. Luckily, I am a person who is not troubled for long when things change. Therefore, I had no difficulty accepting these invitations and entering a situation that was somewhat unclear.

Are you someone who likes to travel first class and stay in five star hotels? Do you enjoy escorted or group trips? This is an important consideration when applying for these programs. When I went to Eritrea, I was entirely on my own in a developing country. I was responsible for getting to the University and back to my hotel, for entertaining myself in the evenings when power failed, and even for getting my laundry done. But opportunities do not exist only for new age Stanleys and Livingstones. There are many programs that send teams to other countries. The point of the above is to stress how important it is to find out in advance what will be expected of you.

Learn about the history of the country you want to visit. History is extremely important–especially in the developing world. Know about the colonial period. Which country was the colonial power to these people? What did they do to and for the country? Understanding this part of a country's history will help you to understand recent history. Eritrea and Uganda are two interesting cases. Both had England as their colonial power but, because of the difference in their treatment by England, there are two different views of the past master.

The people of Uganda, in general, have positive feelings about England and the way it ruled the country. Uganda was the "Pearl of Africa" for the English. A fertile and lush country, it was a luxurious spot for the English to come for a visit and live well. The conditions remained this way until the English disbanded their empire in the early 1960s.

Eritrea, however, is a different story. The people hold England responsible for their lack of infrastructure and thirty years of war with Ethiopia. England thwarted Eritrea's attempt to establish itself as an independent country in 1953 and then facilitated the annexation of Eritrea by Ethiopia. When England departed its Eritrean possession, it also removed much of the heavy industry to Sudan and Egypt. When you understand this, it is easy to see why the Eritrean people have a distrust of most things English.

Related to understanding the history of the country is knowing the current situation. There are many unsettling things happening in the Third World which make safety a concern of all travelers. Anyone considering going to any country should be aware of the situation there. It is wise to begin by reading the State Department Travel Advisories and Consular Information Sheets.[17] These give a cold assessment of the current situation by stating facts and identifying dangerous incidents. The visitor has to read these with care. Evaluate the information by comparing it with current news reports from the area. Finally, potential visitors have to decide for themselves if the risks are worth the benefits of the visit.

The final bit of advice for one venturing on a program such as this–be prepared to be surprised by what you see. You are going to these venues to help them and to share your experience, but do not let this color your view of the people. If you are lucky enough to go to a Third World country, do not assume that a lack of resources equals a backward population. The people are resourceful and value education–they simply do not have the advantages we enjoy in a wealthy society. Be open to learning from these individuals. They will challenge your assumptions about how certain things should be. If you are open to them, you will bring back new ways of looking at your working situation.

People in developing countries lack resources. There is little money for technology and books. Their country's infrastructure may not be able to support electricity twenty-four hours a day. Their roads may be full of potholes. However, despite the lack of what we consider essential infrastructure, there are enormous numbers of very bright individuals trying to elevate their country. Remember, these universities with no textbooks for students and a few thousand books in their libraries still manage to send a tremendous number of graduate students to Europe and the United States for advanced education in top universities. These Third World visitors end up being the top Ph.D. students in these "world class" institutions. Unfortunately, many of them do not return to their home countries. But those who do return instill the idea of the importance of education and growth to their country.

CONCLUSION

My experiences in Eritrea and Uganda were unforgettable and will always be a part of my professional life, even if I fail to have another such opportunity. I feel that I gained much more from the people I went to help than they gained from me. This is a true experience of professional growth.

There are several opportunities each year for librarians of all levels and experiences to participate in these types of visits. Technical service librarians, reference librarians, and computer librarians all have experience and knowledge to share with people in developing countries. You should investigate opportunities that are available through USAID and the Department of State programs and apply.

Library Directors who may be reading this should encourage their staff to look into these types of experiences, encourage them to apply, and, if the applications are successful, make it possible for them to go. The staff member who returns will be an individual who has had a tremendous amount of professional and personal growth and will ultimately help to better the library and its services. From a purely selfish management perspective, this will only reflect well upon you as the Director.

NOTES

1. USAID is an independent federal government agency that receives overall foreign policy guidance from the Secretary of State. The agency works in six principle areas crucial to achieving both sustainable development and advancing U.S. foreign policy objectives: economic growth and agricultural development; population, health and nutrition; democracy and governance; education and training; and humanitarian assistance.

2. Until October 1, 1999, USIA (known as United States Information Service (USIS) overseas) was an independent agency of the U.S. government. On that date, its "public diplomacy" functions, primarily educational and cultural affairs, were transferred to the Department of State.

3. This expansion occurred because of experiences I have had at the University of Maine School of Law. The automation project at the University of Maine involved tying the student records database to our patron database and the use of online ordering, claiming, and payment. In addition to this, I served as Chair for our Admissions Committee and, through that experience, became very familiar with the operation of our parent university's automated administrative systems.

4. The double tragedy of this situation is that the people of Eritrea fought for over thirty years (1961-1993) to establish their independence from the colonial rule of Ethiopia and only enjoyed four years of relatively quiet times before hostilities began again in February 1998.

5. Associate Provost for Technology, Information Systems and Libraries.

6. Among the diverse list of groups I met and spoke with were the Supreme Court of Uganda, the Law Revision Commission, the Parliamentary Library, two legal clinics, the Law Faculty of Makarere University and its Legal Informatics Centre, the East African School of Library and Information Science, the Makarere University Librarians, and the Ugandan Library Association.

7. Between 1962, when Uganda gained its independence, and 1986, when the National Resistance Army led by current President Museveni came to power, the country was the victim of power struggles by many factions. The most internationally known, and infamous, was the eight-year rule of Idi Amin Dada Oumee. The results of his harsh and brutal rule still weigh heavily upon the population of the country today–twenty years after he was deposed.

8. This is not confined to Third World countries–there are many examples of this thinking in universities and governmental offices throughout the United States.

9. *Hansard's Parliamentary Debates.* (In Great Britain this is roughly the equivalent of the *Congressional Record* and has been used generically when referring to similar publications in the countries which previously made up the British Empire.) Prior to the electronic version, there were a limited number of mimeographed copies produced.

10. There has been no case reporting system since the late 1970s.

11. This involved the melding of colonial statutes, military directives from the Amin and Obote years, and traditional tribal traditions into a comprehensive set of modern codes.

12. Kampala 4592, dated 23 September 1999, 0912Z (copy on file with author).

13. *See* note 1, *supra*.

14. *See* Thomas R. French, *Developing Law Library Resources in Eritrea*, Legal Ref. Servs. Q., Vol. 18, No. 3, 2000, at 35.

15. *See* note 2, *supra*.

16. My trip to Eritrea was initiated through a recommendation from Thomas R. French, Associate Law Library Director and Clinical Associate Professor of Law, University of North Carolina School of Law, who had previous experience in Eritrea and who happened to have worked for me at the University of Maine prior to going to North Carolina. My trip to Uganda became a reality after Michael Wolf, American Bar Association African Law Initiative Program, recommended me to various organizations. I met Mr. Wolf on a panel about working in Africa at the 1997 AALL meeting.

17. U.S. State Department, *Travel Warnings & Consular Information Sheets*, *at* http://travel.state.gov/travel_warnings.html (last visited Apr. 5, 2000).

Index

